WORLD IN CONFLICT

KURDISTAN

REGION UNDER SIEGE

KURDISTAN

REGION UNDER SIEGE

by Kari J. Bodnarchuk

Lerner Publications Company / Minneapolis

JA 23 '01

Lerner Publications Company
A division of Lerner Publishing Group
241 First Avenue North
Minneapolis, MN 55401 U.S.A.

Website address: www.lernerbooks.com

Maps pp. 11, 70, and 83 by Philip Schwartzberg, Meridian Mapping, Minneapolis.
Map p. 37 by Laura Westlund.
Cover photo by © Ed Kashi
Table of contents photos (from top to bottom) by © Ed Kashi; The Kurdish Library; The Kurdish
Library; © Ed Kashi; © Ed Kashi.

Series Consultant: Andrew Bell-Fialkoff
Editorial Director: Mary M. Rodgers
Editors: Chris Dall, Lisa K. McCallum
Designer: Michael Tacheny
Photo Researcher: Glenn Marier

LIBRARY OF CONGRESS CATALOGING-IN-PUBLICATION DATA

Bodnarchuk, Kari J.
   Kurdistan : region under siege / by Kari J. Bodnarchuk
    p.   cm. — (World in conflict series)
   Includes index.
   Summary: Presents background information on the Kurds and examines the history of their
ethnic conflict with other peoples in the mountainous regions of southwestern Asia.
   ISBN 0-8225-3556-4 (lib. bdg.)
   1. Kurds—Politics and government—20th century Juvenile literature.
   2. Middle East—Ethnic relations Juvenile literature. [1. Kurds—Politics
and government. 2. Middle East—Ethnic relations]   I. Title.   II. Series.
   DS59.K86B63 2000
   956.6'703—dc21   99-19500

Manufactured in the United States of America
1 2 3 4 5 6 – JR – 05 04 03 02 01 00

CONTENTS

ABOUT THIS SERIES

Government firepower kills 25 protesters . . . . Thousands of refugees flee the country . . . . Rebels attack capital . . . . Racism and rage flare . . . . Fighting breaks out . . . . Peace talks stall . . . . Bombing toll rises to 52 . . . . Slaughter has cost up to 50,000 lives.

Conflicts between people occur across the globe, and we hear about some of the more spectacular and horrific episodes in the news. But since most fighting doesn't directly affect us, we often choose to ignore it. And even if we do take the time to learn about these conflicts—from newspapers, magazines, television news, or radio—we're often left with just a snapshot of the conflict instead of the whole reel of film.

Most news accounts don't tell you the whole story about a conflict, focusing instead on the attention-grabbing events that make the headlines. In addition, news sources may have a preconceived idea about who is right and who is wrong in a conflict. The stories that result often portray one side as the "bad guys" and the other as the "good guys."

The *World in Conflict* series approaches each conflict with the idea that wars and political disputes aren't simply about bullies and victims. Conflicts are complex problems that can often be traced back hundreds of years. The people fighting one another have complicated reasons for doing so. Fighting erupts between groups divided by ethnicity, religion, and nationalism. These groups fight over power, money, territory, control. Sometimes people who just want to go about their own business get caught up in a conflict just because they're there.

These books examine major conflicts around the world, some of which are very bloody and others that haven't involved a lot of violence. They portray the people involved in and affected by conflicts. They describe how each conflict got started, how it developed, and where it stands. The books also outline some of the ways people have tried to end the conflicts. By reading the stories behind the headlines, you will learn some reasons why people hate and fight one another and, in addition, why some people struggle so hard to end conflicts.

WORDS YOU NEED TO KNOW

assimilate: To become part of another culture by absorbing that culture's values and ideas.

autonomous region: An area or territory that is part of a larger political unit but has self-governing powers.

autonomy: The right and power of a region—usually characterized by a shared set of cultural markers, economy, history—to govern itself.

coalition: An association, grouping, or compact formed between the representatives of different interest groups or political parties.

coup d'état: French words meaning "blow to the state" that refer to a swift, sudden overthrow of a government.

de facto government: Meaning "government in fact," an acting authority that may have gained control of a region without going through proper, legal channels.

enclave: A combination of culturally distinct surroundings, whether or not the area or group is enclosed within a foreign country.

ethnic group: A permanent group of people bonded together by a combination of cultural markers, which may include—but are not limited to—race, nationality, tribe, religion, language, customs, and historical origins.

feudal: An economic relationship in which a landowner provides land to a peasant in return for services.

guerrilla: A rebel fighter, usually not associated with an internationally recognized government, who engages in irregular warfare. Membership in a guerrilla group usually indicates radical, aggressive, and unconventional activities.

nationalism: A feeling of loyalty or patriotism toward one's nation, with a primary emphasis on the promotion of a national culture and national interests.

nongovernmental organization (NGO): A private organization that provides aid to people without being affiliated with any particular government. NGOs often provide medical and humanitarian assistance to war-torn regions. NGOs focus on rebuilding and reconciliation in postwar situations.

sanctions: Restrictions, restraints, or embargoes that prohibit or limit trade or diplomatic relations between countries.

self-determination: The free choice, without external compulsion, of a people within a territorial unit to decide their own future political status.

state of emergency: A situation in which the government suspends civil liberties such as freedom of speech, association, or religion in order to deal with a perceived threat to its survival.

treason: The crime of attempting through overt acts to overthrow the government of the state to which the accused owes allegiance.

unilateral cease-fire: When one party in a conflict agrees to cease hostilities without the consent of the other party.

FOREWORD

by Andrew Bell-Fialkoff

Conflicts between various groups are as old as time. Peoples and tribes around the world have fought one another for thousands of years. In fact our history is in great part a succession of wars—between the Greeks and the Persians, the English and the French, the Russians and the Poles, and many others. Not only do states or ethnic groups fight one another, so do followers of different religions—Catholics and Protestants in Northern Ireland, Christians and Muslims in Bosnia, and Buddhists and Hindus in Sri Lanka. Often ethnicity, language, and religion—some of the main distinguishing elements of culture—reinforce one another in characterizing a particular group. For instance, the vast majority of Greeks are Orthodox Christian and speak Greek; most Italians are Roman Catholic and speak Italian. Elsewhere, one cultural aspect predominates. Serbs and Croats speak dialects of the same language but remain separate from one another because most Croats are Catholics and most Serbs are Orthodox Christians. To those two groups, religion is more important than language in defining culture.

We have witnessed an increasing number of conflicts in modern times—why? Three reasons stand out. One is that large empires—such as Austria-Hungary, Ottoman Turkey, several colonial empires with vast holdings in Asia, Africa, and America, and, most recently, the Soviet Union—have collapsed. A look at world maps from 1900, 1950, and 1998 reveals an ever-increasing number of small and medium-sized states. While empires existed, their rulers suppressed many ethnic and religious conflicts. Empires imposed order, and local resentments were mostly directed at the central authority. Inside the borders of empires, populations were multiethnic and often highly mixed. When the empires fell apart, world leaders found it impossible to establish political frontiers that coincided with ethnic boundaries. Different groups often claimed territories inhabited by others. The nations created on the lands of a toppled empire were saddled with acute border and ethnic problems from their very beginnings.

The second reason for more conflicts in modern times stems from the twin ideals of freedom and equality. In the United States, we usually think of freedom as "individual freedom." If we all have equal rights, we are free. But if you are a member of a minority group and feel that you are being discriminated against, your group's rights and freedoms are also important to you. In fact, if you don't have your "group freedom," you don't have full individual freedom either.

After World War I (1914–1918), the allied western nations, under the guidance of U.S. president Woodrow Wilson, tried to satisfy group rights by promoting minority rights. The spread of frantic nationalism in the 1930s, especially among disaffected ethnic minorities, and the catastrophe of World War II (1939–1945) led to a fundamental reassessment of the Wilsonian philosophy. After 1945 group rights were downplayed on the assumption that guaranteeing individual rights would be sufficient. In later decades, the collapse of multiethnic nations like Czechoslovakia, Yugoslavia, and the Soviet Union—coupled with the spread of nationalism in those regions—came as a shock to world leaders. People want democracy and individual rights, but they want their group rights, too. In practice, this means more conflicts and a cycle of secession, as minority ethnic groups seek their own sovereignty and independence.

The fires of conflict are often further stoked by the media, which lavishes glory and attention on independence movements. To fight for freedom is an honor. For every Palestinian who has killed an Israeli, there are hundreds of Kashmiris, Tamils, and Bosnians eager to shoot at their enemies. Newspapers, television and radio news broadcasts, and other media play a vital part in fomenting that sense of honor. They magnify each crisis, glorify rebellion, and help to feed the fire of conflict.

The third factor behind increasing conflict in the world is the social and geographic mobility that modern society enjoys. We can move anywhere we want and can aspire—or so we believe—to be anything we wish. Every day the television tantalizingly dangles the prizes that life can offer. We all want our share. But increased mobility and ambition also mean increased competition, which leads to antagonism. Antagonism often fastens itself to ethnic, racial, or religious differences. If you are an inner-city African American and your local grocer happens to be Korean American, you may see that individual as different from yourself—an intruder—rather than as a person, a neighbor, or a grocer. This same feeling of "us" versus "them" has been part of many an ethnic conflict around the world.

Many conflicts have been contained—even solved—by wise, responsible leadership. But unfortunately, many politicians use citizens' discontent for their own ends. They incite hatred, manipulate voters, and mobilize people against their neighbors. The worst things happen when neighbor turns against neighbor. In Bosnia, in Rwanda, in Lebanon, and in countless other places, people who had lived and worked together and had even intermarried went on a rampage, killing, raping, and robbing one another with gusto. If the appalling carnage teaches us anything, it is that we should stop seeing one another as hostile competitors and enemies and accept one another as people. Most importantly, we should learn to understand why conflicts happen and how they can be prevented. That is why *World in Conflict* is so important—the books in this series will help you understand the history and inner dynamics of some of the most persistent conflicts of modern times. And understanding is the first step to prevention. ⊕

INTRODUCTION

The landlocked, mountainous region known as Kurdistan is located in western Asia, an area that is also known as the Middle East. Covering roughly 230,000 square miles and nearly equal to the size of the state of Texas, Kurdistan is not a country but rather is a region with undefined borders that includes land in Turkey, Syria, Iran, and Iraq. The Kurdish people, also known as the Kurds, have drawn the borders of Kurdistan to encompass territory in which there is a significant Kurdish population. The governments of Turkey, Iran, Iraq, and Syria do not recognize these borders, however.

The Kurds are considered the largest **ethnic group** in the world without a country. For the past century, various Kurdish groups have been fighting for the right to express their cultural identity and to govern themselves. More often than not, this struggle has been met with violence and repression. In particular, tens of thousands of Kurds have been killed and hundreds of thousands have been driven from their homes in Turkey and Iraq over the past few decades. But government repression is not the only obstacle facing the Kurds. The Kurdish fight for freedom and unity has also been repeatedly hampered by differences among the Kurds and by rivalries between different Kurdish groups.

LAND AREA AND TERRAIN

Since Kurdistan doesn't have strictly defined borders, there is no definitive map of the area. The largest section of Kurdistan covers about 80,000 square miles in southeastern Turkey, comprising nearly 30 percent of Turkey's total land. Kurdistan also includes 29,000 square miles of northeastern Iraq (about 17 percent of Iraqi land) and 50,000 square miles of western Iran (about 7.6 percent of Iranian territory). In addition, Kurdistan encompasses a small section of northeastern Syria. The Kurdish territory in Iraq includes an **autonomous region,** where Iraqi Kurds are free to celebrate their culture and practice a certain level of self-rule. There are also Kurdish communities in Central Asia and the Caucasus Mountains.

Facing page: *Kurdistan sprawls across the mountainous area where the borders of Iraq, Turkey, and Iran meet. Although this region holds the highest density of Kurdish people, there are also large Kurdish populations in central Turkey, northeastern Iran, and the Caucasus Mountains.*

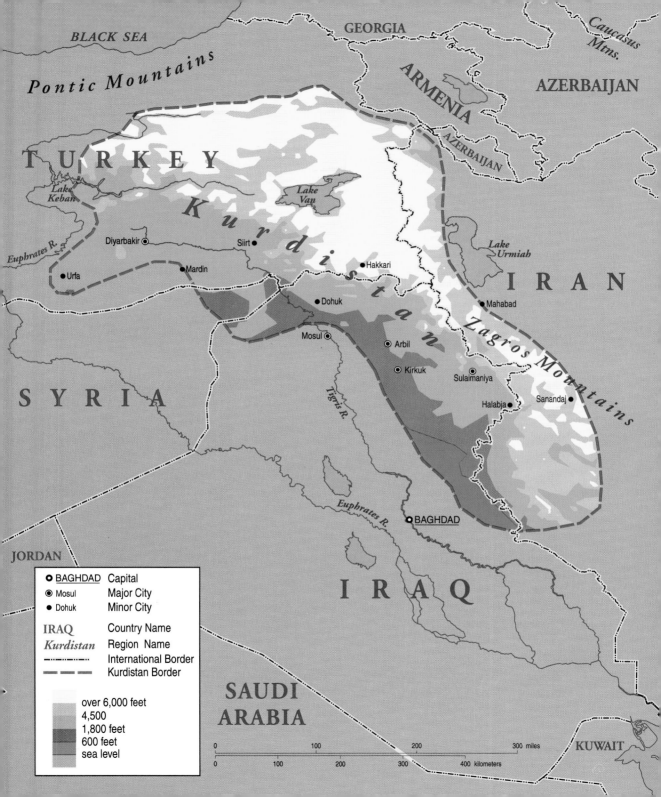

BLACK SEA

GEORGIA

Caucasus Mtns.

Pontic Mountains

ARMENIA

AZERBAIJAN

T U R K E Y

AZERBAIJAN

Lake Keban

Lake Van

K u r d i s t a n

Euphrates R.

Diyarbakir ◉

Siirt ●

Hakkari ●

Lake Urmiah

I R A N

Urfa ●

Mardin ●

Dohuk ●

Mahabad ●

Zagros Mountains

Mosul ◉

Arbil ◉

Kirkuk ●

Sulaimaniya ◉

S Y R I A

Tigris R.

Halabja ●

Sanandaj ●

Euphrates R.

◉ BAGHDAD

JORDAN

I R A Q

○ **BAGHDAD**	Capital
◉ Mosul	Major City
● Dohuk	Minor City
IRAQ	Country Name
Kurdistan	Region Name
––––––––	International Border
– – – – –	Kurdistan Border

over 6,000 feet
4,500
1,800 feet
600 feet
sea level

SAUDI
ARABIA

0   100   200   300 miles

0   100   200   300   400 kilometers

KUWAIT

High mountain peaks provide a dramatic backdrop for this Kurdish village in Turkey. Melting snow and rain feed into the lakes, rivers, and smaller waterways located in Kurdistan and help keep the region fertile.

The landscape of Kurdistan is mainly mountainous. Sections of the Zagros, Taurus, and Pontic mountains are found in Kurdistan. The mountains stretch from southern Turkey into northern Iraq and western Iran. In southern Kurdistan, the mountains slope away into the rolling hills and fertile plains of central Iraq. In eastern Kurdistan the mountains give way to the Plateau of Iran. In the mountains, elevations reach higher than 15,000 feet above sea level. The climate is typically cold and snowy. In southern Turkey, for example, the mountains are covered with snow for six months of the year. The plains and valley regions of Kurdistan generally have a more moderate climate.

The mountains in Kurdistan were at one time heavily forested, but the Kurdish inhabitants have chopped down many of the region's oak, beech, and walnut trees for fuel. Since they don't re-plant after chopping down these trees, the woods have thinned out or completely disappeared in some areas. In addition, demand for timber among the nations of the region and the effects of modern warfare have also stripped Kurdistan of many of its trees. As a result, deforestation, soil erosion, and parched land have become problems in certain sections. But some of Kurdistan's mountains are still blanketed by wild flowers, medicinal herbs, edible vegetables, and stunning waterfalls.

The Tigris and Euphrates rivers—two of the largest and most important rivers in the Middle East—run through Kurdistan. The Tigris River originates in the Kurdish region of Turkey and runs south through Iraq, while the Euphrates River also begins in Turkish Kurdistan and flows southeast across Syria and through Iraq. Both rivers open into the Persian Gulf and provide water to people throughout the Middle East. Water from these rivers is used for farming, transportation, hydroelectric energy, and drinking. Two large lakes—Lake Van and Lake Keban—are located in the Kurdish region of Turkey. Lake Urmiah is a large lake in Iranian Kurdistan.

Although Kurdistan is dotted with many small and remote villages, the region has a number of midsize towns and cities. The main cities or towns in Kurdistan are Diyarbakir, Siirt, Urfa, and Mardin in Turkey; Dohuk, Sinjar, Kirkuk, Sulaimaniyeh, and Arbil in Iraq; and Sanandaj, Mahabad, Bijar, and Kermanshah in Iran. Arbil, which is the capital of the Kurdish autonomous region in Iraq, and Sulaimaniyeh are the two biggest towns in Iraqi Kurdistan, while Diyarbakir has the largest Kurdish population in Turkey's Kurdish region—about 1.3 million Kurds. Kermanshah has the largest Kurdish population in Iran, with about 1 million Kurds.

POPULATION AND DISPLACEMENT

The overall estimated population for Kurdistan ranges

© Ed Kashi

© Christine Osborne Pictures/MEP

Although many Kurds still live in rural villages (left), *cities like Diyarbakir* (above) *have become more crowded since the 1960s. Many Kurds have moved to urban areas to find work.*

from roughly 25 to 30 million. According to the Kurdish Library and Museum in Brooklyn, New York, there were about 30 million Kurds living in Turkey, Iran, Iraq, Syria, and Armenia by the late 1990s. This number represented about 15 percent of the population of the Middle East. The largest Kurdish population is in Turkey, which has more than 15 million Kurds. Between 6 and 7 million Kurds live in Iran, while Iraq is home to 3.5 million Kurds. Syria's Kurdish population is around 1 million. There are about 500,000 Kurds in the former Soviet republics and Russia, and about 1.5 million Kurds scattered throughout the rest of the world.

Since much of Kurdistan is rural and mountainous, many rural Kurds live on steep terrain. They create terraced hillsides (narrow, flat sections of land that look like steps going up the mountains) so that they can use the land for farming. In many regions, they grow tobacco, as well as wheat, barley, rice, and vegetables. About 60 percent of the fruit and 80 percent of the grain produced in Iraq comes from

Iraqi Kurdistan. Cotton and sugar are also important crops. Besides cultivating fields and hillsides, many Kurds raise livestock, such as cattle, goats, and sheep. In fact, Kurdistan provides the majority of these animals for Turkey.

Although traditionally a rural society, the Kurds have become more urban over the past 50 years, both by choice and by force. Part of this population shift has been caused by land reforms and a change to a more industrialized economy. In addition,

the growing use of mechanical farm equipment, which has abolished much of the need for human labor, has put many Kurdish farmers out of work. Although some Kurds have been able to continue working as mechanics or laborers for large landowners, many unemployed Kurds have been forced to look for jobs in urban areas.

Many Kurds, however, have been forced from their villages by the governments of the region. To stifle Kurdish **nationalism** and to keep the Kurds from banding to-

Until the mid-twentieth century, the majority of Kurds were farmers or herders. Many rural Kurds still make their living by working the land or raising sheep and other livestock.

The Kurdish Library

Kurdish Families

Rural Kurdish people, who have large families as a rule, typically live in one-room homes. In these rural families, men tend to do the heavy labor in the fields and go to the villages or cities for supplies. Kurdish women take care of the home and the family and sometimes help plow the fields. Kurdish women in Iran, for instance, must help in the fields, make or mend clothes, iron (using a device filled with hot coals), clean the house, take care of the children, milk the animals, collect water and firewood, and cook for the family. In a society that doesn't have the modern conveniences available in most industrialized nations, this makes for long, hard days.

Some Kurdish children attend school, if there's a school nearby and if they aren't needed to work in the fields. Kurdish boys usually go to school, but girls usually stay home, since girls have to help around the house with chores. In Iran and Turkey, Kurdish children must learn in Persian or Turkish, since the Kurdish language typically isn't taught in these countries.

gether and fighting for control of Kurdish land, the Turkish, Iranian, Iraqi, and Syrian governments have forced the Kurds to leave their homes and move to less populated or less Kurdish areas within their countries. Some have expelled Kurds from their countries altogether. Turkey in particular has tried for decades to force the Kurds to forget or deny their Kurdish heritage and to **assimilate** into the society in which they live, while Iraq and Syria have forcibly removed Kurds from their homes.

The effect of this popula-tion movement on Kurdish settlement patterns is clear. In 1965 about 28 percent of the Turkish Kurds lived in rural towns, and 72 percent lived in small villages. Within the next 30 years, hundreds of thousands of Kurds had moved to large cities and towns in Turkey. According to a census taken in 1990, about 51 percent of the Kurdish population in Turkey lived in urban settings. Istanbul, in western Turkey, had 2.5 million Kurds by 1990—the largest number of Kurds in any city in the world. The population of Diyarbakir, a predominantly Kurdish town, grew from about 380,000 in 1991 to 1.3 million by 1996. Similar migrations occurred in Iran and Iraq. Swelling populations within the cities have led to housing and job shortages, increased crime and disease, and conflicts between Kurds and the original city dwellers.

The displacement and forced assimilation of the Kurdish people, particularly in Turkey and Iraq, make it difficult to calculate how many Kurds actually exist and where they live. Many Kurds, especially those living in Turkey, are afraid to admit

A Kurdish family in Turkey dances at a Kurdish wedding ceremony. The groom has money pinned to his suit. Despite the Turkish government's attempts to force assimilation, many Kurds have kept traditional practices alive.

they're Kurdish because they fear punishment by the government. The number of Kurds living in Kurdistan is also uncertain because the Kurdish nationalist groups—those who support Kurdish self-rule—tend to inflate the numbers to help their cause. At the same time, the governments in Turkey, Iran, Iraq, and Syria have been known to minimize Kurdish population statistics.

KURDISH CULTURE

The Kurds evolved over thousands of years from a mixture of cultures that settled in the Middle East. During this time, the Kurds developed a language and a culture that made them a distinct group. Physically similar to other Middle Eastern groups, the Kurds are distinguished by their culture rather than by racial or ethnic characteristics.

Historically, the Kurds in Turkey, Iraq, Iran, Syria, and elsewhere shared a similar lifestyle—a nomadic, tribal existence based on agriculture and the raising of livestock. Kurdish men have a reputation as fierce and brave warriors. Kurdish traditional dress is colorful and flamboyant. The Kurds are very fond of music, dance, poetry, and storytelling.

Kurdish literature and folk songs celebrate this shared culture. The Kurds also celebrate a common holiday—Newroz, the Kurdish new year—on the first day of spring.

Like most people in the Middle East, the majority of Kurds are Muslim, which means they practice the Islamic faith. The Islamic religion is divided into two main branches, called Shiite and Sunni. The majority of Kurds in northern Iraq are Sunni Muslims. The Kurds of Turkey, Iran, and Syria are also predominantly Sunni Muslim. But some Kurds also practice the Jewish and Christian faiths, while a small number follow the ancient Kurdish religion called Yezidism, which combines traditions of Islam, Christianity, Judaism, and other Middle Eastern faiths. A few

Kurds practice the Alevi and Al-I-Haqq religions.

One of the Kurds' distinguishing characteristics is their language, an Indo-European language that is related to Persian. The two main dialects of this language are Kurmanji, spoken by Kurds in northern and north central Kurdistan, and Sorani, spoken by Kurds in the south. In addition, there are many different dialects and subdialects of Kurdish. The Kurds also use different alphabets, depending on where they live in the Middle East. The Kurds of Iran and Iraq use an Arabic alphabet, while the Kurds of Turkey and Syria use a Latin alphabet. Kurds living in Armenia use a Cyrillic alphabet. As a result, the Kurds are the only ethnic group in the Middle East without a unified language. These language barriers can make communication between Kurds and efforts to unite them difficult. The lack of a unifying language also enables some governments in the region to deny a distinctly Kurdish identity.

SOCIAL STRUCTURE

Another shared trait is social structure. Until the second half of the twentieth century, the social structure in Kurdistan was mainly tribal. Traditionally each rural tribe contained about 20 to 30 families, called clans, that formed a cohesive group based on common ancestry. Clans in rural communities and villages farmed the land and raised livestock. The land, including pastures, was often owned by the entire tribe, but each clan was in charge of cultivating a plot of land. During harvesttime, clans pooled resources and joined together to harvest the fields and share the crops.

The tribal system was the basis of Kurdish society until World War I (1914–1918), when the Kurdish regions of the Ottoman Empire (1453–1923) were divided to create the borders of modern-day Turkey, as well as the new states of Iraq and Syria. Although tribalism is not as strong as it once was, it's still an important aspect of Kurdish life and politics. Many rural Kurds still belong to a tribe or clan and follow the governing of tribal leaders. Since Kurdistan doesn't have a national government, tribal leaders are the closest thing they have to political authority. Kurds who have moved to more urban areas generally do not adhere to the tribal structure, and they view the world much differently than do rural Kurds with strong tribal affiliations.

In modern-day rural Kurdish society, tribal members are connected more by allegiance than by blood ties. These alliances are typically found in **feudal** villages, where families aren't related to each other or the landowner or leader. The landowner in the village collects taxes from those who work the land, and the workers, in turn, receive access to land for cultivation. The workers also get to keep a portion of what is produced. Each individual must belong to a household or family to be part of a village. The needs of the family and the village take precedence over an individual's needs, since survival depends on the success of the group.

Relationships between tribal members tend to be very close. Tribalism—with its community atmosphere and sense of security, self-interest, and self-preservation—has enabled groups of Kurds to survive throughout the years. Members of a tribe are loyal to one another and to their leader. But tribalism has also caused Kurdistan to remain very divided, since there is rivalry between Kurdish tribal leaders. These leaders have exerted a lot of energy fighting each other for power, rather than joining forces and fighting for Kurdish **autonomy** or independence.

THE KURDISH STRUGGLE

The Kurds have been fighting for some form of **self-determination** for the past century. Ultimately, many Kurds would like to see the creation of an independent Kurdistan. But because there is strong opposition to a Kurdish state among the nations of the region, the Kurds have had to aim for more realistic goals. Nearly all Kurds believe that they should have the right to express their cultural identity, including the right to speak, write, and publish in Kurdish. Many Kurds also believe that, as a separate and distinct group, the Kurds should be granted autonomy within their respective countries. The Kurds face a great deal of resistance in their attempt to gain such rights.

There are several reasons for this resistance. The Kurds are predominantly located in Turkey, Iraq, Iran, and Syria. Except for Iran, these states were established in the early part of the twentieth century from the remnants of the multiethnic Ottoman Empire. As these new countries developed, their governments tried to create a sense of national identity through unity, which meant establishing homogenous societies where only one identity could be expressed. To maintain these societies, each government has violently suppressed minority groups and forced minority peoples to assimilate.

Since the Kurds are the most conspicuous minority group asserting their cultural and national rights, they are the biggest target of suppression. The governments in Turkey, Iran, Iraq, and Syria believe that if the Kurds are given autonomy, other ethnic groups will begin making the same demands, thereby dividing the countries even more and possibly leading to their dismemberment. Although all four countries have had conflicts with one another, they are united in the belief that the Kurds should not break away and form their own country, state, or government in the Middle East.

Each government deals with the Kurds in different ways. The Turkish government believes that a Turkish nation should consist of Turkish citizens who celebrate a Turkish culture and support Turkish unity. If Turkey allows different groups to fight for and demand cultural freedom or national independence, the government believes the country will lose its sense of uniqueness and solidarity, as well as its strength as a na-

> *The governments in Turkey, Iran, Iraq, and Syria believe that if the Kurds are given autonomy, other ethnic groups will begin making the same demands, thereby dividing the countries even more and possibly leading to their dismemberment.*

The Importance of Resources

No nation wishes to give away land, to diminish its size, its population, or its resources—the elements that help a nation define itself. Countries with Kurdish populations are no different. Kurdish land runs continuously through Turkey, Iraq, Syria, and Iran. All of these countries fear that if the Kurds in one country get political control over Kurdish territory in that country, the Kurds in another country will be encouraged to demand the same control. Turkey and Iraq, in particular, fear losing territory that contains two of the region's most vital resources—oil and water.

For much of the twentieth century, the presence of oil in the Kurdish region of Iraq has played a role in the Iraqi Kurds' struggle for autonomy. Oil is a major part of the Iraqi economy, responsible for more than 90 percent of the nation's foreign income. From the 1960s through the early 1990s, the shipment of oil to other countries earned money for the Iraqi government, allowing it to import food, industrial and agricultural equipment, and consumer items. Most importantly, oil income enabled the Iraqis to build a large army and become a regional power. For these reasons, controlling the country's oil is a high priority for the Iraqi government, which suppresses the Kurdish autonomy movement and seeks to replace the Kurds in these areas with Arab citizens.

The abundant sources of water in Turkish Kurdistan are to the Turkish government what oil is to the Iraqi government. The countries of the Middle East desperately need water for crop irrigation. As a result, some leaders believe that water will be the key issue in the Middle East in the twenty-first century. The two most prominent sources of water in the region are the Tigris and Euphrates rivers, which begin in Turkey. Through a series of dams, the Turkish government controls the amount of water that flows into Syria and Iraq. Control of this vital resource gives Turkey a great deal of leverage over these countries.

tion. As a result, Turkish leaders have tried to suppress and even deny Kurdish identity.

Turkish Kurds are denied the right to fair trials, free speech, and civil liberties. They are forbidden from wearing Kurdish clothes and speaking Kurdish freely. Although Turkish Kurds can speak Kurdish in social situations, it is illegal for them to educate their children in Kurdish, to broadcast radio or television programs and print newspapers in Kurdish, and to use Kurdish in political dialogue. Some Kurds have been arrested and forced to perform hard labor because they were caught speaking Kurdish in political forums. The Turks use military force to stifle and suppress Kurds living in the mostly Kurdish provinces of southeastern Turkey.

In Iran, a multiethnic society that is made up mostly of Persians but also includes, Kurds, Arabs, Azeris, Baluchis, and Turkomans, there has been little chance for the Kurds to gain greater cultural freedom or autonomy. The Iranian government believes that Persian culture should be dominant. Iran fears that if it gives the Kurds more cultural and political rights—including autonomy—other minority groups in the country will ask for more rights, too. The government believes this would lead to a collapse of Iranian culture and unity. As a result, Kurds and other non-Persian groups have always been referred to as Iranians. The government grants the Kurds only limited cultural rights and has maintained a ban on the Kurdish language.

In Iraq, a nation whose population is 75 percent Arab, President Saddam Hussein and the ruling Baath Party want to maintain the predominance of Arab people and Arab culture. Although the Iraqi government recognizes the Kurds as Iraqi citizens and grants them cultural freedom, it suppresses Kurdish efforts to gain control of Kurdish territory in Iraq. In addition to using military force to quell Kurdish nationalism, the Iraqi government has also forcibly removed Kurdish citizens from their villages and replaced them with Arab citizens—a process known as Arabization.

Syria has the smallest Kurdish population in the Middle East. The Kurds represent only about 8 percent of the total population in Syria. The Kurds, a repressed minority, have been denied cultural, political, and economic freedoms. Syrian President Hafiz al Assad has followed the tactics of the Turkish government by trying to force the Kurds to assimilate into Syrian society. He has also banned Kurdish political parties. Until 1978, the government instituted an Arabization project similar to Iraq's, during which Kurds were expelled from their homes and replaced with Arabs.

GROUPS INVOLVED IN THE KURDISH CONFLICT

There are a number of groups fighting for the Kurdish cause in the Middle East, but these groups are more divided than united. The reasons for this are numerous. Kurdistan encompasses many different geographical locations and tribal affiliations, as well as linguistic and socioeconomic backgrounds. In addition, Kurds living in different regions often speak a different dialect of Kurdish and use different alphabets, which complicates the effort to establish a unified language. Finally, the Kurds are spread across sections of four nations in the Middle East, in mountainous regions where the weather conditions are often very harsh and travel is difficult.

The main groups involved in the Kurdish conflict can be divided by country, although the whereabouts of these groups frequently shift as they move across borders, build new bases and dissolve others, and are expelled from countries in which they operate. In Turkey the Partia Karkaren Kurdistan (PKK), which means Kurdistan Workers Party, is a Kurdish political group whose goal is to gain autonomy within Turkey. This group, led by Abdullah Ocalan, is fighting for political, economic, and cultural freedom for the Kurds and believes that it is humiliating for the Kurds to be denied the right to speak Kurdish and practice Kurdish customs.

The PKK's main opponents are the Turkish government—led by President Suleyman Demirel, who took office in 1993, and Prime Minister Bülent Ecevit, who stepped into office in 1996— and the Turkish military. The government and the military, two separate entities with different ideas but somewhat similar goals, view the PKK as a terrorist group that poses a major threat to the stability of Turkey and the safety of Turkish citizens. Neither the government nor the military admit that there is a Kurdish problem in Turkey.

The main Kurdish political parties in Iraq are the Kurdistan Democratic Party (KDP), which is run by Massoud Barzani, and the Patriotic Union of Kurdistan (PUK), led by Jalal Talabani. Both groups have fought for Kurdish autonomy within Iraq, but they have also fought each other. The KDP and the PUK share control of an autonomous Kurdish **enclave** in northern Iraq. In 1992 members of both groups were elected to form a body—called the Kurdish Regional Assembly—to govern the region. But since that election, the rival PUK and KDP parties have battled each other for control of the region. Their biggest mutual opponent is the Iraqi government, which has often used brutal methods to suppress the Kurds and prevent them from gaining control of Kurdish territory in Iraq.

The main Kurdish group in Iran is the Kurdistan Democratic Party of Iran (KDPI), which is the largest of the Kurdish opposition groups. Founded in the late 1940s, the KDPI has long been pressing for an autonomous region within a democratic Iran. The KDPI leadership is mainly comprised of urban Kurds, but the group's fighting force is drawn from rural Kurds. Opposing the KDPI is the government of Iran, which is run by Shiite Muslims who view the Sunni Kurds as a separatist threat. Although the Iranian government does grant the Kurds limited cultural rights, the Iranian military has attacked Kurdish communities in northern Iran and has assassinated KDPI leaders.

The Kurdish nationalist movement in Syria isn't as active as it is in Turkey, Iraq, and Iran. In Syria the Kurds form a relatively small percentage of the total population and are divided geographically, living mainly in three separate regions. Kurdish political organizations are also illegal in Syria, although there are a few that reportedly have limited legal status. These groups can, for instance, oversee Kurdish Newroz celebrations and file complaints if Kurdish land is confiscated. But they cannot condemn or criticize the Syrian government, its policies, or its political parties. In addition, Syrian leader Hafiz al Assad is known for his brutality in suppressing opponents of his government. As a result, Syrian Kurds have not played a prominent role in the Kurdish struggle. Were they to do so, they would face imprisonment at the very least.

The focal point of the Kurdish struggle is the mountainous region where Turkey, Iran, and Iraq meet. The Kurdish groups in these countries have clashed with each other, as well as with the governments and military forces of these nations over the past century. Although this struggle rarely makes international headlines, it has caused major disruptions in a region that has seen its share of conflicts. ⊕

MAJOR PLAYERS IN THE CONFLICT

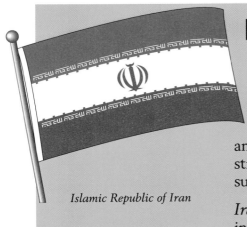

Islamic Republic of Iran

Iran, Islamic Republic of Home to nearly 7 million Kurds, who live in the northwestern part of the country. The government of Iran, which is run by Shiite Muslims, grants Iranian Kurds limited cultural and political rights. The Iranian military maintains a strong presence in the Kurdish regions of the country to suppress Kurdish nationalism.

Iraq, Republic of Home to 3.5 million Kurds, who live in the northern part of the country. Iraqi leader Saddam Hussein has launched numerous military campaigns against the Kurds to destroy their campaign for autonomy and to maintain control of the oil-rich land in the region. The Iraqi government has also forcibly removed Kurdish civilians from their homes in order to disperse the Kurdish population.

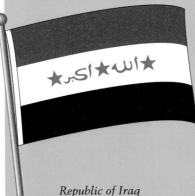

Republic of Iraq

Kurdistan Democratic Party (KDP) A political and military group that fights for Kurdish autonomy within Iraq. The KDP shares control of the Kurdish enclave in northern Iraq with the Patriotic Union of Kurdistan (PUK). Founded by Massoud Barzani, the KDP has fought for Kurdish autonomy since the early 1950s.

Kurdistan Democratic Party of Iran (KDPI) The largest of the Kurdish opposition groups, the KDPI has been pressing for Kurdish autonomy within Iran since the 1940s.

Massoud Barzani

Abdullah Ocalan Leader of the Partia Karkaren Kurdistan (PKK—also called the Kurdistan Workers Party) Since 1984, Ocalan has directed the PKK's war against the Turkish government from neighboring Syria.

Partia Karkaren Kurdistan (PKK—also called the Kurdistan Workers Party) The PKK is a political and military organization that has been engaged in an armed conflict with the Turkish military since 1984. Led by Abdullah Ocalan—who runs the organization from Syria—the PKK consists of a political wing and a guerrilla force. Although the PKK originally fought for Kurdish independence, these days the group seeks autonomy within Turkey and greater cultural rights for Turkish Kurds.

Patriotic Union of Kurdistan (PUK) Led by Jalal Talabani, the PUK is a political and military organization that fights for Kurdish autonomy in Iraq and shares control of the Kurdish enclave in northern Iraq with the KDP. In recent years, the PUK and the KDP have fought one another for supremacy in northern Iraq.

Turkey, Republic of Home to more than 15 million Kurds, who live in the southeastern part of the country. Since becoming a republic in 1923, Turkey has suppressed its Kurdish population by banning expressions of Kurdish culture and forcing Kurdish civilians to assimilate into Turkish society. Since 1984 the Turkish military has been fighting a war against the PKK in southeastern Turkey.

Abdullah Ocalan

Jalal Talabani

Republic of Turkey

CHAPTER 1

THE RECENT CONFLICT AND ITS EFFECTS

In a small village in southeastern Turkey, groups of Kurdish children play while others head off to school or to the fields. Their parents spend most of their day cultivating the land, growing food, and caring for the family. Occasionally, the family is forced to give some of their food to PKK **guerrillas,** who are battling the Turkish army for control of the region. The family might not support the PKK's armed struggle, but they do support the fight for Kurdish freedom. They look forward to the day when their children are allowed to speak Kurdish in school, when they can read a local newspaper written in Kurdish, and when they can openly celebrate their ethnicity. But those freedoms probably won't be granted in the foreseeable future.

The PKK has gained a large and loyal following among the Kurds of southeastern Turkey. The group is made up of young men and women from the Kurdish region of Turkey who have seen their people suffer under Turkish law and the Turkish soldiers

© Ed Kashi

A Kurdish family waits for Turkish commandos to search the area for PKK guerrillas.

> *Many Kurds choose to leave rather than fight against their own people. But when Kurdish villagers refuse to become village guards, they're forced to leave their schools, their jobs, and most of their belongings.*

who enforce it. They have joined the rebel group to fight for Kurdish rights and for Kurdish autonomy within Turkey. Supporters of the PKK—which was established by Abdullah Ocalan in 1978 and began guerrilla operations against the Turkish government in 1984—view the group as the only protection against Turkish repression. The Turkish government and military, on the other hand, view the PKK as a terrorist group.

One day, Turkish troops arrive in the village and demand that the Kurdish family help them fight the PKK. The Turkish soldiers say that the PKK is disrupting the peace and unity of the country. These soldiers continually visit the village to encourage or force residents to become village guards, who serve as watchdogs in the village. The Turkish army typically pays these guards a fee—sometimes quite a lot of money—to monitor the area, suppress uprisings, prevent villagers from aiding the PKK, and fight against PKK guerrillas. The soldiers leave the Kurdish villagers with two choices—take up arms against the PKK or leave the village.

Many Kurds choose to leave rather than fight against their own people. But when Kurdish villagers refuse to become village guards, they're forced to leave their schools, their jobs, and most of their belongings. The Turkish army will probably burn everything they leave behind. This is just one tactic the army uses to punish the PKK and those who support it. Sometimes the Turkish soldiers attack and destroy Kurdish villages in their quest to hunt down PKK fighters. They drive out and kill those believed to be members of the PKK. Meanwhile, local police forces, with the help of village guards, arrest and torture Kurds who are thought to be aiding the PKK.

The PKK has responded to this violence with their own violence, attacking Turkish soldiers and killing Kurds who become village guards or act as government informants. Sometimes, PKK fighters kill family members of village guards as a warning to others. The PKK has also been accused of killing innocent civilians. The Turkish government claims this is terrorism, but the PKK views these acts as retaliation against an oppressive government and army.

VIOLENCE IN TURKEY

The conflict between the PKK and Turkish security forces—which include local police forces, the Turkish army, and Kurdish village guards—has been going on for nearly 15 years. It is estimated that Turkey uses billions of dollars in foreign aid, at least 20 percent of its annual budget, and hundreds of thousands of Turkish troops each year to fight the PKK. During the 1990s, Turkey sent up to 400,000 troops to battle PKK members in Turkey and northern

Many PKK guerrillas (left) *train in the Bekaa Valley of Lebanon and in Syria. Led by Abdullah Ocalan* (below), *the PKK has been fighting the Turkish government since 1984.*

Iraq, where the PKK had established bases. By the end of 1997, at least 37,000 people had been killed in the conflict between the Turkish security forces and the PKK. About 3,000 Kurdish villages had been destroyed in Turkey and up to 2 million Kurds had been displaced. Despite the financial and human cost, Turkey remained determined to eliminate the PKK.

In 1998 the Turkish army continued its quest to defeat the PKK by force. In March 1998, Turkish forces launched a major offensive in southeastern Turkey to eliminate PKK guerrillas, who were trying to reorganize after a harsh winter in the mountains. In late April 1998, about 40,000 Turkish troops attacked villages in southeastern Turkey to find and kill PKK guerrillas. Soon afterward, Turkish forces led a large-scale assault on PKK rebels around the Kurdish city of Diyarbakir. Throughout the year, the Turkish military deployed troops to Kurdish areas in the southeastern section of the country. Meanwhile, Turkish security forces arrested, tortured, and killed Kurdish civilians during security sweeps.

Many human rights advocacy groups, such as Human Rights Watch and Amnesty

International, as well as politicians in the United States and Europe, feel that the violent actions of the Turkish security forces are extreme. They believe that Turkey has committed numerous human rights violations against innocent civilians. Between 1993 and 1996, human rights groups filed more than 4,000 complaints against Turkey for violating the human rights of its citizens. The U.S. State Department's annual Country Report on Human Rights Practices claimed that Kurdish civilians were frequently tortured by Turkish security forces. The report detailed how Turkish troops abused Kurdish civilians and Kurdish guerrillas by suspending these people by their arms, depriving them of sleep, beating and raping them, and subjecting them to electric shocks.

Nevertheless, Turkish leaders deny that they've engaged in any wrongdoing and claim the human rights accusations made against them are false. These leaders assert that they are fighting a war against a terrorist group that commits violent acts against innocent civilians, including Kurds. Their goals are to put a stop to PKK terrorism, to bring a sense of stability back to the Kurdish region of Turkey, and to preserve Turkish unity. Turkish government and military leaders claim that the PKK has committed numerous human rights violations.

As the PKK and Turkish forces battle, the Kurdish civilians who are caught in the middle of the struggle suffer the most. Many Kurdish civilians live in constant fear for their personal safety. Women and children are particularly vulnerable to the violence and abuse. When Turkish troops raid Kurdish villages, many of the men are often away fighting. The women and children are the only people left in the villages, so they are the ones the Turkish soldiers harass and terrorize. The women

Turkish Censorship

Although the U.S. State Department and human rights agencies release annual reports on Turkey and its human rights record, people in the United States aren't always aware of what's going on in Turkey. One of the main reasons why they know little about events in Turkey is because of Turkey's Anti-Terror Law, which prohibits free speech if it threatens the nation's unity. Although the Turkish press can cover a wide range of subjects without restriction, the Turkish government does have limits when it comes to certain "sensitive" topics. As a result, Turkish journalists who write candidly and honestly about Turkey's treatment of the Kurds often face prosecution. Since the Anti-Terror Law was enacted, hundreds of journalists covering the Kurdish conflict have been fined, imprisoned, and tortured. In fact, by the mid-1990s, about 15 Turkish journalists had been killed for their reporting on Turkey's human rights abuses. Foreign correspondents have been affected by this law as well. For instance, Aliza Marcus, a correspondent for Reuters, has been prosecuted for stories she has written about Turkey's treatment of the Kurds. As a result of Turkish censorship, readers in the United States and around the world know little about Turkey's treatment of its Kurdish population.

are often beaten, jailed, and tortured because they support or are connected with members of the PKK. The conflict also disrupts the lives of the Kurds on the most basic level. For instance, when the Turks put an embargo on southeastern Turkey to keep Kurdish civilians from feeding PKK members, citizens were forced to use certificates to obtain food each day.

The Turkish government suppresses the Kurdish population in other ways. Ten provinces in southeastern Turkey have been under a **state of emergency** since 1987. The state of emergency decree enables the regional governor of these provinces to put restrictions on the press and to remove people deemed dangerous. The regional governor has used this power to forcibly remove Kurdish civilians from their villages. Then there is the country's Anti-Terror Law, which was established by Turkish president Turgut Ozal in 1992. This law prohibits free speech if it threatens the unity of Turkey. The government has used the law to close down Kurdish newspapers, ban Kurdish books, prevent Kurdish performers from singing in Kurdish on public stages, and arrest Kurdish rights activists.

KURDS IN IRAQ AND IRAN

Meanwhile, in the Kurdish autonomous region in northern Iraq, the KDP and the PUK have been fighting the government of Iraq. Unlike Kurds living in Turkey, Kurds in Iraq are allowed to express their cultural identity. But for decades the Kurds in Iraq have been fighting to gain political control over their territory. The government of Saddam Hussein doesn't want to give up Kurdish land because the oil found in the

© Ed Kashi

Bombardments by the Iraqi army have leveled many cities in Iraqi Kurdistan (facing page), leaving civilians to fend for themselves in often harsh conditions (right).

© Ed Kashi

Kurdish region of Iraq is important to the Iraqi economy. Hussein's troops have used brutal methods to control the Kurds, including chemical weapons attacks that have wiped out whole towns. But the Kurds of northern Iraq—led by the KDP and the PUK—have persevered.

Kurdish resistance in northern Iraq has been plagued by factionalism, however. When the KDP and the PUK aren't fighting the Iraqi government, they are fighting each other for control of northern Iraq. They also struggle over profits earned from smuggling goods across the Turkish border and from trading diesel fuel with Turkey. Several thousand PUK and KDP members have been killed during the fighting between these two groups. In addition, each group has intimidated, threatened, and killed Kurdish civilians in northern Iraq to gain support.

The most recent fighting between the two groups occurred in late August 1996, in the mountainous regions near the town of Rawanduz, along the Iran-Iraq border. KDP leader Massoud Barzani and PUK leader Jalal Talabani were struggling with each other for power and control over the Kurdish autonomous region. When the fighting erupted, the PUK asked the government of Iran for support and the KDP received assistance from the government of Iraq—the same government that had suppressed the Kurds earlier. The Iraq-KDP offensive helped the KDP win territory from the PUK, but it also forced thousands of Kurds to flee to refugee camps in Iran.

As the PUK and the KDP fought for control of the protected enclave, Kurdish civilians in northern Iraq suffered. As a result of the Iraqi government's embargo on northern Iraq, which prevented the Iraqi Kurds from receiving food and medical supplies, unemployment rose and the number of crops produced in the region dropped. In 1995 the Food and Agriculture Organization (FAO) and World Food Program (WFP) released a report on the conditions among the 2.1 million people in Iraqi Kurdistan. According to the report, the FAO and WFP found that "schools, hospitals, water and sanitation systems, and government buildings have been damaged or looted. Discontinuation of electricity supply to (Arbil) governorate has adversely affected water supply and public health services. Potable water is only available to a small fraction of the inhabitants of (Arbil) city. Blood banks have been rendered unusable as have been medicines and vaccines that require refrigeration."

The UN claimed that the majority of people in Iraq were living below the poverty level and that more than 50 percent of the women and children in Kurdistan were getting less than half the daily calories needed to remain healthy. Children had suffered the most be-

Kurds in the Caucasus

There are an estimated half-million Kurds living the countries of Armenia and Azerbaijan, two former Soviet republics that lie in the Caucasus Mountains. The largest Kurdish cities in the Caucasus are Lachin and Kelbajar, located in Nagorno-Karabakh, a disputed region that lies in Azerbaijan. Like many of the Central Asian republics that used to be under Soviet rule, Azerbaijan and Armenia have experienced their share of ethnic conflict. The Kurdish residents of Nagorno-Karabakh have been one of the victims of this conflict.

The trouble began in the late 1980s, when ethnic Armenians (known as Karabakhis) in Nagorno-Karabakh began demanding independence from Azerbaijan. A full-fledged war started when the enclave seceded from Azerbaijan. By 1994 Karabakhi fighters, aided by Armenian troops, had taken control of the region. In the process of defeating Azeri troops, the Karabakhis removed most of the non-Armenian population, including Kurds, from the area. Most of those Kurds ended up in refugee camps in Azerbaijan.

cause of the war. By 1996 about 22 percent of the children were stunted or small for their age, due to lack of food and proper nutrition. The food shortages were caused, in part, by a lack of seeds, fertilizers, and pesticides necessary to produce essential crops. The World Health Organization (WHO) and UNICEF were working together to provide better health for Kurds, especially women and children. Aid agencies worked to alleviate the suffering, but they were

facing their own problems as well. Many groups had been forced out of the area when fighting between the PUK and KDP broke out.

PKK activity in northern Iraq has added to the problem. Since they began their fight against the Turkish government, PKK rebels have sought a safe haven in northern Iraq. The KDP and PUK, who see the PKK as a threat to their own control over the region, blame the group for trying to exert control over Iraqi Kurdistan against the will of the Kurds living there. Both parties claim that PKK fighters have been responsible for kidnapping, torturing, and killing Iraqi Kurdish civilians, interfering with humanitarian efforts in northern Iraq, and damaging the property and crops of Kurds in this region. Since 1991 the PUK and the KDP have been aiding Turkey by closing the border of northern Iraq to PKK rebels and by actively supporting Turkey's military efforts against the PKK. As a reward, Turkey has assured the KDP and the PUK that they will be given control over the Kurdish region of northern Iraq.

Meanwhile, in Iran, another Kurdish group—the KDPI—has also been fighting for the Kurdish cause. But the assassination of KDPI leaders by the Iranian government has prevented the organization from gaining much headway. In 1996 the KDPI received support from the Iranian Kurdish Communist Party and the PUK in its attempt to overthrow the Iranian government. But when the independence movement failed, leaders of these Kurdish groups fled the country. Throughout the 1990s, Iranian troops have maintained a strong presence in Iran's Kurdish regions.

KURDS AGAINST KURDS

Recent events show that the governments of Turkey, Iraq, and Iran use extreme force to deal with the Kurds and the Kurdish nationalist movement. But recent disputes between the KDP, PUK, and the PKK highlight

The fighting force of the KDP and the PUK is made up of soldiers called peshmergas. *These fighters range in age from boys in their teens to men in their fifties.*

© Ed Kashi

Kurdish exiles in London perform a traditional dance.

Kurdish Refugees

In addition to the Kurdish population in the Middle East, there are nearly two million Kurds spread throughout Europe, North America, and Australia. Germany has one of the largest Kurdish populations outside of the Middle East, with nearly 500,000 Kurdish residents. France, Britain, and Italy also have significant Kurdish populations. Accurate population numbers for European Kurds are hard to come by, however, because European governments often list Kurdish people as Turkish, Iranian, or Iraqi citizens. In the United States, many Kurdish Americans live in California, Texas, and New York.

Kurdish refugees often face difficult journeys. In recent years, Kurds who have been forced from their villages in Turkey have fled the country and have been transported by boat illegally to countries such as Greece and Italy. In 1997 more than 3,500 Turkish Kurds escaped by boat to Italy, where they sought political asylum or continued on their journeys to other European countries, such as Germany and France, to join relatives. Thousands more Kurds came to Italy in 1998. Many Iraqi Kurds have also headed to Europe by boat. These voyages are often dangerous. Sometimes the boats run aground; other times they get caught in storms and capsize.

Wherever they end up, expatriate Kurds typically live close to other Kurds and join Kurdish organizations. This solidarity helps Kurdish refugees adapt to their new countries and maintain their heritage at the same time. Many expatriate Kurds are also involved in organizations that advocate the Kurdish cause and promote Kurdish language and culture. For example MED-TV, a television station that broadcasts Kurdish language programming throughout Europe, operates from London. Some Kurdish groups in Europe, however, have recently been accused of sending money to the PKK and of recruiting and training people to fight for the organization. As a result, European governments are keeping a watchful eye on these groups. The extent of Kurdish political activity in Europe became evident in February 1999, when Kurds throughout Europe protested the arrest of Abdullah Ocalan.

another problem that has haunted the Kurds throughout their history—infighting among Kurdish political parties. Intra-Kurd disputes have been one of the biggest obstacles in the Kurds' fight for political freedom.

Kurdish groups have often fought against each other instead of joining forces to fight toward a common goal. They have a habit of breaking alliances and joining forces with their enemies to fight against fellow Kurds. The tendency of Kurdish groups to seek the most beneficial alliance for themselves has been one of the reasons why the Kurds have failed to gain political freedom. If a Kurdish leader tells his group they'll be better off if they fight against another Kurdish group, his supporters will rise up against that group. As a result, the different Kurdish factions have continually betrayed, murdered, and oppressed each other during their struggle.

A look at recent history reveals the tendency of Kurdish factions to link forces with any group—even their enemies—as long as it's a mutually beneficial arrangement. The KDP has joined

The Kurdish national motto, with origins older than anyone can remember, is simply: "The Kurds have no friends."

forces and made agreements with the PKK, the PUK, the Turkish government, and the Iraqi government upon occasion—but has fought these very same groups at other times. The same is true with the PUK, which has negotiated agreements with or solicited support from the Iraqi government, the Iranian government, the Turkish government, and the PKK, as well as the United States and Israel. Meanwhile, the PKK has solicited support from the KDP, the PUK, the Iraqi government, the Iranian government, the Syrian government, and the Armenian government.

While the governments of Iran, Iraq, and Turkey fight and suppress Kurdish movements in their own countries, they eagerly support each other's Kurdish groups. But they do so mainly to antagonize each other and to exploit the divisions in Kurdish society. For instance, Iran has supported the PUK and the

KDP in Iraq, to weaken the Iraqi government. Similarly, Syria has provided a haven for the PKK to antagonize Turkey. And the Turkish government has supported the Kurdish parties in northern Iraq, in return for their help in stopping the PKK.

The mistreatment of the Kurdish people by their host countries, and the tendency for Kurdish groups to fight one another are not new phenomena. Throughout the history of the region this pattern has repeated itself. Examining the history of the Kurdish people and the history of the nations that suppress Kurdish aspirations will help to explain the current dilemma. ⊕

CHAPTER 2
THE CONFLICT'S ROOTS

Unlike many modern ethnic groups, the Kurds did not descend directly from one particular group of people. Most scholars believe that the ancestors of the Kurds came from many different groups of people, some of whom settled in what has become the modern-day region of Kurdistan as long as 12,000 years ago. One of the first groups to inhabit what would become Kurdistan was the Halafians, who came to the region in 6000 B.C. The Hurrians, a group that migrated to the region around 4300 B.C., established the Kurds' native religion—Yezidism—and social structure. In 2000 B.C., groups of people speaking Indo-European languages began to slowly migrate into the region from Europe and Asia and overtake the Hurrians. Three of the largest clans of these Indo-European people were the Medes, the

The area that would become Kurdistan was home to a number of early civilizations. The domestication of animals such as sheep and goats began in this region. The Kurds formed nomadic tribes led by aghas, or tribal chiefs, who roamed these rolling hills in a constant search for grazing land.

Scythians, and the Persians. Over many centuries, the Kurdish people emerged from this mix of cultures.

By 300 B.C., a number of small Kurdish kingdoms had sprung up in the mountainous region that straddles the borders of what have be-

come Turkey, Iraq, Iran, and Syria. But the Romans overtook the kingdoms in the western part of this region during the first century B.C., while the Persian Empire claimed the eastern half in the third century A.D. In the seventh century A.D., the

Saladin

Sultan Saladin, or Salah al-Din Yusuf ibn Ayyub, was an important figure in the Crusades, a series of eight Christian military expeditions organized to recapture Palestine from the Muslims. European Christians called Palestine the Holy Land, the place where Jesus had lived and died. Saladin's recapture of the city of Jerusalem in Palestine from the Crusaders in 1187 resulted in the Third Crusade, which was led by Richard, King of England. Richard's attempt to recapture the city failed, but Saladin let Christian pilgrims enter Jerusalem after negotiating a treaty.

North Wind Picture Archive

Sultan Saladin recaptured Jerusalem for the Muslims in 1187.

Arabs—a group that practiced the Islamic faith—came to the region from what would become Saudi Arabia, taking land as they swept through. Slowly, the Kurds joined forces with the Arabs and accepted the Islamic religion.

Under Arab rule called the caliphate, the Kurds established numerous independent dynasties and developed their own distinct culture. A pastoral, nomadic people who moved from place to place in search of grazing land for their herds, the Kurds organized themselves into tribes, which encompassed people of common ancestry. Kurdish tribes, headed by *aghas* (tribal chiefs), were able to function independently on a local level, even though the Arabs controlled large sections of Middle Eastern territory. The Arabs thought of the Kurds as good soldiers, and Arab leaders often used Kurdish fighters in their armies. At times, the Kurdish tribes supported the Arab caliphate and joined in its battles against other regional powers, such as the Armenians, Persians, and Byzantines. At other times, the tribes rose up against the empire. Internal fighting within tribes was also common, as the more powerful Kurdish aghas struggled for control of people and territory.

One of the most legendary Kurds was Sultan Saladin, who lived during the twelfth century. He fought for the Islamic religion and founded the Ayyubid dynasty, which ruled Egypt and Syria from the late twelfth century through the middle of the thirteenth century. As head of the Ayyubid dynasty, Saladin built schools, canals, and mosques and supported theologians and scholars.

CAUGHT BETWEEN EMPIRES

In the late twelfth century, Emir Osman, the leader of

The army of the Ottoman Empire quickly established itself as a dominant force in the Middle East. Eventually Ottoman power extended into Kurdistan.

Cultural and Tourism Office of the Turkish Embassy

nomadic Turkish tribes from Central Asia, inherited a small kingdom in Anatolia (modern-day Turkey). By the late fifteenth century, this kingdom had grown to become the Ottoman Empire, which included all of Anatolia and parts of southeastern Europe. At the turn of the sixteenth century, Shah Is-mail—the head of an Azeri family known as the Safavids—established the Safavid dynasty in Persia (modern-day Iran). Both powers vied for territory in the region. In addition, the Ottomans, who practiced the Sunni version of the Is-lamic faith, disagreed about religious issues with the Safavids, who practiced the Shiite version. Kurdish tribes, located in the mountains between the two empires, ended up between the warring powers.

Between 1505 and 1508, Shah Ismail's troops fought their way westward and captured territory in Mesopotamia (modern-day

Iraq), including Baghdad and the mostly Kurdish cities of Diyarbakir and Mosul. Then he and his forces incited anti-Ottoman uprisings among tribes in eastern and central Anatolia. A decisive battle occurred in 1514, when the Ottoman's new sultan, Selim, and his army defeated Shah Ismail at Chaldiran, just northwest of Lake Urmiah. The Ottoman victory led to the division of the Kurdish region, leaving the Ottomans in control of Kurdish territory in Anatolia and the Persians ruling Kurdish land in Azerbaijan. After the battle at Chaldiran, the majority of Kurds sided with the Ottomans. The Kurds joined forces with the Ottomans because the two groups shared the Sunni Muslim faith. The Kurds were also impressed by the Ottomans' military strength.

The Ottomans divided their Kurdish territory into three main *vilayets*, or provinces. The Kurds and Ottomans then signed the Kurdo-Ottoman pact, which split a portion of the Kurdish region into 16 independent territories, or emirates. Each emirate was ruled by a family, with one member of the family appointed to be emir. The Ottomans gave Kurdish emirs in southern Kurdistan full freedom to govern these regions. The emirs didn't have to pay a tribute to the

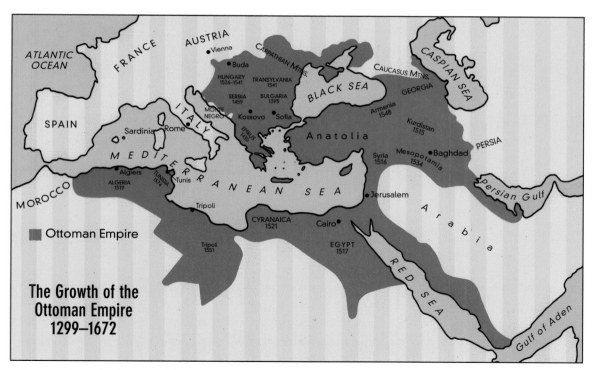

The Growth of the Ottoman Empire 1299–1672

This map shows the division of the Middle East between the Ottoman Empire and Persia. Kurdistan straddled the dividing line between the two powers.

> *At this point, Kurdish tribes were more focused on gaining power than on joining with other Kurdish tribes to form a united group.*

Ottoman sultan or live under his rules, but they agreed to police the regions and offer military support whenever necessary. The rest of the Kurdish territory was divided into *sanjaks*—feudal estates ruled by Kurdish aghas who also guaranteed loyalty and military support to the sultan. For the Kurds, this arrangement provided an appealing balance between imperial and local government.

Meanwhile, the shah wanted direct control over Persia's Kurdish tribes, so he appointed Persian or Turkoman administrators to govern the Kurdish regions in Persia. But the Kurdish tribes enjoyed a sizable degree of independence because the administrators were too far away to enforce their authority over the region.

The Kurds maintained a certain amount of independence during this period and played an important role in the struggle between the Ottomans and the Persians.

Kurdish tribes were often involved in battles between the two empires. The Kurds located along border areas sided with either power, depending on which alliance was more beneficial to them. Their choices weren't necessarily based on true allegiance to a group. Instead, Kurdish tribes typically chose to fight with whoever had the best chance of winning.

This era also witnessed power and territory struggles between Kurdish tribes in the region. In some cases, Kurdish tribes would enlist Ottoman or Persian support to defeat a rival tribe. At this point, Kurdish tribes were more focused on gaining power than on joining with other Kurdish tribes to form a united group. Despite this, the relative independence enjoyed by the Kurdish tribes enabled a distinctive Kurdish culture to blossom. Kurdish literature and art thrived, and Kurdish cities became important cultural centers. Many modern-day Kurds view this period as the Kurdish renaissance.

CHALLENGING OTTOMAN AUTHORITY

By the beginning of the nineteenth century, the power of the Ottoman Empire had begun to decline. The empire had grown so large that it was becoming difficult to rule. Local rulers, especially the Kurdish emirs and aghas, had so much freedom that they often ignored the wishes of the central government. To retain and regain control over this territory, the Ottomans began stripping power from Kurdish leaders and asserting direct rule. In addition, the Ottomans looked to the Kurds to provide military support against the Russians and the Persians, who coveted Ottoman land.

Kurdish tribal leaders were opposed to this new policy. They viewed Ottoman attempts to assert imperial authority and to force the Kurds to fight for the sultan as a threat to their own power. The Kurdish population also resented the fact that Ottoman battles against

During the nineteenth century, Kurdish tribes led numerous rebellions, such as the one shown (right), *to break free of Ottoman control.*

KURDS CHARGING.

North Wind Picture Archive

the Russians and the Persians took place within Kurdish territory, leaving villages and land destroyed. In response to these trends, the Kurds fought to loosen themselves from the tight grip of the Ottomans, gain back more power, and retain their feudal rights.

During the first half of the nineteenth century, Kurdish emirs and aghas led several revolts against the Ottomans. The first of these revolts occurred in 1806, when Kurds in the principality of Baban took up arms for three years before being crushed by the Ottomans. Other uprisings followed in 1826, 1828, 1840, 1847, and 1855. Some Kurdish groups and leaders used the continuing Persian-Ottoman conflict to their

advantage and increased their attacks on the Ottomans. They hoped Ottoman forces would be weakened by the war with Persia and less focussed on the Kurds. Some Kurds provided support to the Russians when they fought the Ottomans in 1828, 1854, and 1877.

Although Kurdish tribes found common cause in fighting to regain control of their territory, many of the revolts ended with tribes turning against one another, as tribal leaders chose to fight for supremacy rather than for Kurdish independence. Some tribes even

fought with Ottoman forces against other Kurdish tribes. The inability of the tribes to unify helped the Ottomans suppress these revolts. By 1867 the Ottoman Empire had completed its goals of wiping out the autonomous Kurdish principalities, reducing the power of Kurdish leaders, and establishing direct rule over Kurdish territory.

The Persians did not clash as much with the Kurds in their region, but they did face a major revolt in 1880, when Sheikh Ubaidullah, the Persian Kurds' spiritual leader and mediator, rose up to challenge the authority of

Sheikh Ubaidullah

The Ottoman leadership's removal of the Kurdish emirs had unsettling repercussions for Kurdish society. The emirs had often acted as mediators between different tribes, helping to peacefully solve disputes over land. Without the calming influence of the emirs, Kurdish tribes fought constantly and disrupted trade in the region. The Ottoman governors could do little to prevent the upheavals.

Religious leaders known as sheikhs gradually filled the role of mediator in Kurdish society. One of the most popular sheikhs was Sheikh Ubaidullah of Shamdinan, who was supported by Kurds in Ottoman and Persian territory. The sheikh supported the establishment of a Kurdish nation. There was talk that the Armenians would be getting their own independent state and the sheikh wanted to make sure the Kurds weren't forgotten or dismissed.

In 1880 Sheikh Ubaidullah and his sons led a rebellion against Persia after the shah's local governors had punished Kurdish tribal chiefs. Ubaidullah hoped that the revolt would lead to an independent Kurdistan. Overlooking his endorsement of Kurdish nationalism, the Ottomans supported the sheikh against their Persian rivals. During the revolt, Kurdish forces gained control of a large area between Lake Urmiah and Lake Van. When the Persians fought back, the sheikh looked to the Ottomans for support but didn't receive any. The Kurds in the Ottoman territory helped as much as they could, but they had to protect their own land. The sheikh then asked for help from the Russians, but they also refused to lend a hand.

Eventually, Ottoman and Persian armies crushed the sheikh's revolt with the help of rival Kurdish tribes. The Ottomans assisted the Persians because they feared that Sheikh Ubaidullah was growing too powerful. His forces fled, were captured, or were killed. The sheikh was exiled and died in Hejaz, Saudi Arabia, in 1883.

the Persian shah. Despite gaining the support of Ottoman and Persian Kurds, this uprising was eventually put down by Ottoman and Persian forces.

Despite the Ottomans' attempts to control their empire, they could not prevent its decline. Russia, France, and several other nations sought to gain access to Ottoman land. In addition, the Armenians, a Christian group in Ottoman territory, were trying to gain independence from the empire.

At this point, the Ottomans turned to the Kurds for help. The Ottomans realized that they could use the Kurds' help to fight those who were trying to take land from the empire. To gain Kurdish support, the Ottoman leaders began giving land to the Kurdish upper classes, exempting Kurds from taxation, and offering education for the sons of tribal chiefs. They also made appeals to Muslim unity. The Ottomans hoped that strengthening the Kurds' ties to the central government would not only secure the eastern edges of the empire but also end Kurdish dissension.

In 1891 Ottoman sultan Abd al Hamid II founded a cavalry group called the Hamidieh, consisting of groups of men from various Kurdish tribes. Each regiment included men from a single tribe, with the tribal chief as leader. The function of the Hamidieh was to defend the Ottoman Empire from the Russians and to suppress any expressions of Armenian independence. The cavalry group also functioned to generate Kurdish support for the sultan, especially among Kurds living along the border regions between the Ottoman and Persian Empires. The Ottomans offered a number of incentives to attract potential members, including special training, smart-looking uniforms, and educational opportunities for members' children. The sultan ended up using the Hamidieh regiments to violently quash Armenian uprisings in eastern Anatolia from 1894 to 1896. But the Hamidieh also put down Kurdish revolts as well.

THE RISE OF NATIONALISM

Despite Ottoman attempts to integrate the Kurds into the empire and to stifle Kurdish desire for independence, the Ottomans could not contain the rise of Kurdish nationalism. In the 1890s, groups of young, educated Kurdish aristocrats and military officers became more active in voicing and supporting Kurdish issues. In 1898 Midhad Bedir Khan Bey founded the first Kurdish journal, an educational and cultural publication called *Kurdistan* that was translated into Turkish as well. The Ottoman authorities forced the publication out of the country when it became a platform for Kurdish patriots.

The rise in national consciousness among educated Kurdish aristocrats was helped along by political events occurring in the empire. In 1902 a group of nationalist military officers— opposed to the despotic rule of Sultan Abd al Hamid II and fed up with watching the dissolution of the empire—

formed a new secularist (nonreligious) group called the Young Turk Decentralization Party. The Young Turks believed that the future of the Turkish people lay in a Turkish state. The Young Turks also wanted equality for all Ottoman subjects, whether or not they were Muslims. In 1908 the Young Turks led a military **coup d'état,** known as the Young Turk Revolution. A year later, the Young Turks deposed the Ottoman sultan, and the Committee of Union and Progress (CUP) took over the leadership of the empire. The CUP called for equality among all the empire's citizens.

The Kurds rejoiced. Many Kurds supported the Young Turks during the revolution, hoping to benefit from their leadership. Taking advantage of the political change, Kurdish leaders Emir Ali Bedir Khan Bey, General Sharif Pasha, and Sheikh Abdul Qaydr formed Taali we Terrakii Kurdistan (Recovery and Progress of Kurdistan), the first Kurdish political organization. The group published a journal—in Turkish only— called the *Kurdish Mutual Aid and Progress Gazette,*

Despite Ottoman attempts to integrate the Kurds into the empire and stifle Kurdish desire for independence, the Ottomans could not contain the rise of Kurdish nationalism.

which discussed issues of Kurdish culture, language, and identity. At the same time, young Kurdish intellectuals and patriots established clubs in eastern Anatolia. Awareness of Kurdish identity was growing among the Kurdish population.

The Kurdish political movement was short lived, however. CUP members and Turkish nationalists came to view the presence of Kurdish and other non-Turkish groups as a threat to Turkish strength and economic prosperity. Some even regarded minorities as a threat to Turkey's existence, since independence movements by various ethnic groups had already led to the loss of Ottoman territory. A year after the CUP started, it abandoned its decision to include non-Turkish groups and began banning Greek, Bulgarian, and Kurdish groups and organizations. It banned all non-Turkish publications, schools, clubs, and associations, including those that were Kurdish. The CUP also took steps to curb the power of Kurdish tribal chiefs and sheikhs.

The Turks' new political stance sparked Kurdish revolts in the countryside and led to the establishment of a number of secret Kurdish clubs. One of the first clandestine clubs, called Kurdish Hope, was created in 1910 by Kurdish students and intellectuals.

In 1913 Kurdish Hope began printing a bilingual Kurdish-Turkish daily paper called *Roja Kurd* (Kurdish Sun), which carried articles on Kurdish nationalism and the Kurdish alphabet. This publication helped keep the Kurdish language alive. Kurdish Hope wasn't supporting a fully independent state for the Kurds; it did, however, favor Kurdish autonomy and equal rights for Kurdish people.

WORLD WAR I

World War I brought about massive changes in the political structure of the Middle

Kurdish Nationalism

As Kurdish nationalism grew within the Ottoman Empire in the late nineteenth and early twentieth century, two separate and distinct lines of thought began to emerge. Some Kurds, known as autonomists, believed that the Kurdish people were equal to Turks and other Ottoman subjects and should be treated as such. They didn't demand that the Kurds should have their own nation but did want to have equal representation in the Ottoman government. For the autonomists, maintaining cultural and political ties to the empire was as important as being able to proclaim their Kurdish identity. Others Kurds, called secessionists, wanted complete Kurdish independence. The gulf between these two groups prevented the formation of a unified Kurdish movement. The growth of Kurdish nationalism caused other divisions among the Kurds. Kurdish nationalism was particularly strong among urban, liberal Kurds. Tribal chiefs and sheikhs in rural Kurdistan, who feared losing their traditional power, felt threatened by the liberals' attempts to promote literacy and to increase political awareness. Without the support of these traditional leaders, Kurdish nationalism failed to spread among rural Kurds, who formed the majority of the Kurdish population.

Kurdish troops helped the Ottoman army defend eastern Anatolia against Russian and Armenian forces.

East. In 1915 the Ottoman Empire joined forces with Germany and Austria-Hungary and fought against the allied countries of Britain, France, the United States, and Russia. CUP leaders were hoping to renew the Ottoman Empire, but the British, French, and Russians were interested in dividing up the Ottoman territory among themselves. The CUP was also faced with a number of ethnic groups—including the Kurds, Arabs, and Armenians—who wanted independence.

The Russians, who hoped to annex all of the Kurdish regions in eastern Anatolia, were the greatest threat to the Turks. Russian leaders, promising military aid and support for Kurdish independence, convinced some Kurds to support them against the Turks. But most Kurds joined the Turks. CUP leaders appealed to the Kurds by reminding them of their religious and political ties to the empire. The Kurds paid a heavy price for their role. In one instance, Russian troops visited a Kurdish village and killed nearly nine-tenths of its population.

The Kurds were not the only group to suffer. In fact, they played a significant role in suppressing another group seeking independence. When the Armenians called on the Russians for support, the

The Fourteen Points developed by Woodrow Wilson were intended as a guide for a peace settlement to World War I. Point Twelve called for giving nationalities under Turkish rule the opportunity for self-government.

Special Collections and Archives, Rutgers University Libraries

CUP enlisted Kurdish forces to kill or displace them. In 1914 and 1915, Kurdish fighters—believing they would gain future support, more rights, and possibly land—helped massacre and expel Armenians in eastern Anatolia. Bands of Kurds traveled to Armenian villages, where they raped women and children, tortured men and pregnant women, and stole women for slavery. More than one million Armenians died in the war.

But the Kurds received no benefits for their role. The CUP had always intended to use the Kurds to fight the Russians and to drive the Armenians from eastern Anatolia. With this accomplished, Turkish leaders planned to displace the Kurds by moving them to western Anatolia and spreading them out. Their goal was to break down Kurdish nationalism, which they feared was still growing. In 1917 the CUP ordered the resettlement of about 700,000 Kurds. It is believed that as many as half of these people might have died in the process.

Although the Ottomans' defense of their eastern border was successful, the rest of the war did not go as well. British and Arab forces captured Ottoman territory in Palestine, on the Arabian peninsula, and in Mesopotamia, while Greek, French, and Italian forces occupied Turkish land along the coast of the Aegean Sea. As the war came to an end, CUP leaders went into hiding, leaving the Ottoman sultan to sign a peace agreement with the allied powers, who hoped to carve off large sections of the empire and establish new states under their control. Eventually, the CUP, led by General Mustafa Kemal, established a Turkish national movement in opposition to the sultan and the allied occupation.

HOPES FOR INDEPENDENCE

The collapse of the Ottoman Empire provided the Kurds with one of their best chances to become an independent nation. In 1918 the United States sent the King-Crane Commission to the Middle East to come up with suggestions for the future of the region. The commission recommended that one-fourth of the land inhabited by the Kurds be established as an independent Kurdish state and that a portion of the old Ottoman territory be given to the Armenians, so that they, too, could set up their own state.

That year, U.S. president Woodrow Wilson drew up the Fourteen Points Declaration. Point Twelve dealt with the future of the region formerly under control of the Ottoman Empire, stating that, "The Turkish portions of the present Ottoman Empire should be assured a secure sovereignty, but other nationalities which are now under Turkish rule should be assured an undoubted security of life and an absolutely unmolested opportunity of autonomous development." This suggested that the Turks were guaranteed a sovereign state and that other minority ethnic groups in the region—like the Kurds and the Armenians—would be able to pursue autonomy. Turkish Kurds established committees and organizations to voice support for Kurdish independence.

Although for the Kurds this statement seemed promising, it made no real guarantees for a Kurdish nation. It also posed a threat to the Turks, who didn't want to hand any of their land over to other ethnic groups. General Sharif Pasha, a Kurdish leader in exile in France, voiced concerns that the Turks would try to pit the Kurds and the Armenians against each other to wipe out the Armenians and then

European Motives

Despite the lofty rhetoric of Woodrow Wilson's Fourteen Points Declaration, the allied powers were more concerned about gaining access to Ottoman land and building their empires than guaranteeing independence for the Kurds, Arabs, or any other ethnic group. In fact, the Europeans were trying to determine the fate of the region before the war ended.

In 1916 the foreign ministers of Britain and France, Sir Mark Sykes and Georges Picot, signed the Sykes-Picot Agreement, which laid out a plan for the division of the Arab regions of the Ottoman Empire between France, Britain, Greece, Italy, and Russia. France and Britain hoped to establish dependent states and spheres of influence in the region. France got control of the mostly Kurdish province of Mosul. By the end of the war, the British were occupying the province and were determined to hold on to it. The French agreed to give up Mosul, then demanded renegotiations. The San Remo Pact, signed in December 1920, was the outcome of the new plan. This pact gave France nearly 24 percent of the shares of oil earned by the British-owned Turkish Petroleum Company. The Sykes-Picot Agreement set the stage for the Sèvres Treaty, in which much of Kurdistan was divided between the British and French, leaving the Kurds only a small area of land. For Britain and France, an autonomous Kurdistan served a strategic purpose. Both countries hoped that a small Kurdish state would act as a buffer against the Turks. The situation changed when the Turks rejected the treaty and fought to regain the land that the Allies had taken during the war. To secure a peace agreement with the Turks and keep their territory, the Allies were willing to give up all demands for Kurdish independence.

eliminate any opportunities for Kurdish autonomy. In addition, the Kurds didn't have any central leadership to spearhead a campaign for a nation of their own.

The Kurds were caught between competing interests. The British, who coveted Kurdish land in Mesopotamia for its recently discovered oil deposits, worked hard to gain the support of Kurdish tribes in Anatolia, telling Kurdish leaders that they would promote the creation of an independent Kurdistan out of the Kurdish regions in southeastern Anatolia. The Turks also appealed to Kurdish tribes, traveling to Kurdish villages and holding talks with influential tribal leaders. The Turks warned the Kurds that if they were under European control, they might be punished for their past crimes against the Armenians. Emphasizing Ottoman and Muslim unity, Mustafa Kemal successfully urged the Kurds to help the Turks fight the allied occupation. And, as Pasha had warned, Kemal pitted the Kurds against the Armenians.

Meanwhile, in the British-controlled provinces of Basra, Baghdad, and Mosul—

which had previously been under Ottoman rule—Kurdish tribes were in revolt. British administrators had concluded that it would be impossible to establish a self-administered Kurdish state in the region because it was too underdeveloped and communication was poor. The decision angered the Kurds and resulted in attacks against British officers. The uprisings were led by Sheikh Mahmoud Berezendji, a well-respected Kurdish chief. In May 1919, the sheikh

gathered 300 followers and captured British personnel. Other Kurds soon supported his efforts and the sheikh declared himself ruler of the Kurds. But British soldiers eventually caught and exiled the sheikh, ending the rebellion and solidifying British rule.

By 1919 there were three different views among the Kurds of the Ottoman Empire. Some were supportive of the Allies, others favored the Turks, and a third group wanted complete indepen-

Although the European powers stated their support for an independent Kurdistan, they were more concerned with dividing the Ottoman Empire among themselves.

dence without any ties to other countries. Many others, however, did not know which view to support.

KURDISH HOPES DASHED

At the 1919 Paris peace conference—held to finalize the settlement of the war—the British and French discussed the issue of Kurdish autonomy. The two European powers agreed that the Kurds didn't have a political system or a national policy that would enable them to run their own independent nation. But since the British didn't want to lose their territory in the Kurdish sections of Mesopotamia, they suggested that a Kurdish state be established in southeastern Anatolia.

When the Paris conference ended in August 1920, the Ottoman sultan and the allied powers signed the Treaty of Sèvres, which completely carved up the Ottoman Empire. The treaty left the Turks with Istanbul and parts of Anatolia, while the Armenians, Greeks, French, and British took the rest of Ottoman land. The treaty also announced that Britain, France, and Italy would set up a commission to help

By 1919 there were three different views among the Kurds of the Ottoman Empire. Some were supportive of the Allies, others favored the Turks, and a third group wanted complete independence without any ties to other countries.

oversee the establishment of an autonomous Kurdistan. It stated that if, after one year, the Kurds still wanted to become an independent nation and the League of Nations, an international body formed to resolve disputes, agreed that the Kurds could effectively run their own affairs, the Kurdish region would become fully independent. The treaty stipulated that the Turks and the allied powers would have to agree on the Kurds' ability to run their own nation.

Although this sounded like a victory for the Kurds, the proposed Kurdish region was a small mountainous area encompassing Kurdish territory in southeastern Anatolia and northern Mesopotamia. The area lacked much of the fertile land that had originally been part of the Kurdish territory. In fact, it represented only one-third of the territory inhabited by Kurdish

people. And even though the oil-rich vilayet of Mosul would be located in the proposed Kurdish region, it would actually remain under British control. The small Kurdish state would be bordered by a French-ruled territory to the west, Persia to the east, the new Armenian state to the north, and the new state of Syria to the south.

In the end, however, the treaty was never implemented. After agreeing to the peace deal, the Ottoman government fell and was replaced by a provisional government under Mustafa Kemal. Just days before the final signing of the treaty, the new Turkish government announced that it would not agree to the terms of the treaty. Kemal said he wouldn't go along with anything the Ottoman government had endorsed.

As a result of this, the Sèvres treaty was discarded.

Kurdish men gather at a crowded marketplace in Kurdistan in 1919. After the war, the Kurds were hopeful that an independent Kurdistan would be established. That hope eventually faded as the Turks and the British maneuvered to gain control of Kurdish land.

Meanwhile, Kemal and the Turks continued to fight the occupation of Turkish land, battling the Greeks in the west and the Armenians in the east. Again the Kurds were split. Some tribes fought with Kemal, who promised to create a Turkish republic in which Kurds and Turks would have equal rights. Others rose up against Kemal with the support of the British. Both powers used the Kurds to achieve their goals. Kemal hoped to win back land—including Kurdish territory—lost during the war and to establish a Turkish nation. Kemal and his forces defeated the Greeks and Armenians and regained control of Anatolia.

THE STRUGGLE FOR MOSUL

Meanwhile, Kurdish tribes in the British-controlled territory of Mesopotamia were fighting another battle. In 1920 a League of Nations mandate (order) granted Britain control of the provinces of Basra and Baghdad. Under the terms of the mandate, the British were responsible for establishing an Arab government and for preparing the territory for independence. In 1921 the British chose Emir Faisal, who had been leader of the Arab revolt against the Ottomans, to be the first king of the Kingdom of Iraq. The new nation included the vilayet of Mosul, which was populated mostly by Kurds. But the Kurds didn't want to be part of an Arab state, and between 1920 and 1922, Kurdish tribes in Iraq revolted against the British.

The Iraqi Kurds were aided by the Turks, who sought to reclaim the oil-rich vilayet of Mosul for themselves. Since the British wanted Mosul to remain under their control, they tried to convince the Kurds that Britain would better serve Kurdish interests. Believing they needed a figure to gather the support of the Kurdish tribes, the British brought Sheikh Mahmoud Berezendji from exile and asked him to be the governor of this region. Then, as part of the 1922 Anglo-Iraqi Treaty—which promised independence for Iraq in 10 years—the British and King Faisal offered the Iraqi Kurds the right to set up an autonomous region. They hoped that the promise of autonomy would lure the Kurds away from the Turks.

Sheikh Mahmoud had other ideas, however. Instead of following British directions, he gathered support from other tribal leaders and declared an independent Kurdistan, proclaiming himself "King of Kurdistan." Under the sheikh's leadership, Kurdish tribes again rose in revolt, attacking and killing several British soldiers north of Mosul. The Turks encouraged these Kurdish uprisings to push the British out of the area, and the British retaliated by sending planes to bomb the Kurds. When Britain reneged on its promises and turned down the Kurds' requests for autonomy in 1923, Sheikh Mahmoud again gathered troops. But eventually, British troops toppled Sheikh Mahmoud and sent him into exile in Persia. Still, he continued to lead raids and cause trouble in tribal regions along the border of Persia and Iraq.

Persia was also experiencing Kurdish uprisings during this time. Spurred on by the Kurdish revolt under Sheikh Mahmoud, Agha Simko, the leader of the Kurdish tribe the Abdui Shikak, gained a substantial section of land in western Persia and threatened the government's control of the region. But in 1923, General Reza Khan, a Persian cavalry officer, led a coup to overthrow the ruling Qajar dynasty. He then led a military expedition against

Reza Kahn (above) *and Mustafa Kemal* (right), *later known as Atatürk*

Simko and his supporters, who were driven into Iraq.

THE TREATY OF LAUSANNE

In July 1923, European powers drew up the Treaty of Lausanne to take the place of the discarded Treaty of Sèvres. The new treaty, signed and ratified in August 1923, declared Turkey a republic and established it as the main landholder of the Kurdish territories, with 43 percent. The treaty divided the remaining Kurdish territory between Persia, Iraq, Syria, and the newly formed Soviet Union. There was no mention of autonomous Kurdish or Armenian states or of Kurdish rights. In Turkey, Syria, Iraq, and Persia, the Kurds became second-class citizens.

After the signing of the treaty, Turkish president Mustafa Kemal—who had become known as Atatürk (Father of the Turks)—went back on all of the promises he had made to the Kurds. In fact, Turkey stripped the Kurds and other minorities in Turkey of all rights. Atatürk forbade the Kurds from speaking their own language, learning Kurdish in school, or publicly acknowledging that a Kurdish culture even existed. All Kurdish books, magazines, newspapers, and literature were banned. To keep the outside world from learning about

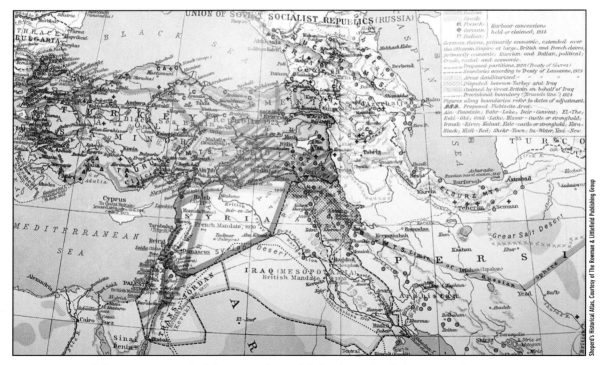

After all the peace treaties had been signed, Kurdish land was divided among Turkey, Iraq, Syria, Persia, and the Soviet Union.

the cultural restrictions placed on the Kurds and other minorities, Atatürk declared Turkish Kurdistan a military area. No foreigners were allowed to enter. He even had the stories of Kurdish origins rewritten, so that people would believe the Kurds had descended from the Turks.

Atatürk's goal was to make Turkey a state with only one nationality—Turkish. All other nationalist groups were denied legitimacy and forced to assimilate. Atatürk feared that the Kurds would threaten Turkey's national security if they asserted their cultural identity and tried to establish a Kurdish state. He believed that Turkey's social unrest and economic problems were caused by minorities, especially the Kurds, Greeks, and Armenians. Kemal aimed to unify the country, ethnically and religiously, through repression.

The Kurds of Persia faced a similar situation. Like Atatürk, Persian leader Reza Khan planned to turn his country into a homogenous nation by crushing any sense of ethnic identity among the various groups living there. In fact, he wanted to entirely

> From this point on, Turkey's active repression of the Kurdish population became commonplace. The Kurds were frequently subjected to martial law, massacres, displacement, and the destruction of their villages.

eliminate tribalism in Persia. Because Persia was made up of many different ethnic groups—Azeris, Turks, Arabs, Kurds, and Baluchis—he sought to create a unified Persian culture rather than attempt to wipe out all non-Persian groups, which would have been impossible.

KURDISH INSURRECTIONS

In reaction to Turkish repression, Sheikh Said of Piran, a Kurdish agha, led a massive revolt in 1925, aimed at asserting Kurdish rights and establishing an independent Kurdistan. During the uprising, Kurdish forces captured the town of Darhini and declared it the capital of Kurdistan. Other rebellions took place around Turkish Kurdistan, and eventually Kurdish rebels seized one-third of the region.

When the Turkish government in Ankara realized the scope of the Kurdish upris-

ing, it imposed martial law throughout the Kurdish provinces. To stop the Kurdish leaders and to retake the territory, the government sent 80,000 troops to the region. The Turkish air force devastated the Kurds during bombing attacks. The Turkish army eventually reclaimed the region, killing thousands of peasants, burning hundreds of villages, and hanging about 400 Kurdish patriots in the process.

In March 1925, Turkey's new prime minister, Ismet Inonu, established the Law for the Restoration of Order. This law granted the Turkish government the power to execute people who incited, encouraged, or led rebellions, as well as those who disrupted the "tranquility or social harmony" within Turkey. As a result, the government executed Sheikh Said and about 660 other Kurds believed to have participated in the rebellion. About 7,500 others were arrested as suspects for involvement in the revolt.

From this point on, Turkey's active repression of the Kurds became commonplace. The Kurds were frequently subjected to martial law, massacres, displacement, and the destruction of their villages. To break up tribes and to discourage Kurdish nationalism, the Turkish military displaced nearly one million Kurds from their villages. Thousands of Kurds died from lack of food, warmth, and supplies when the Turks forced them from their homes during the winter of 1925. Others, including Kurdish nationalists who had not taken part in the revolt, were massacred by Turkish troops.

But the Kurdish uprisings did not end. In early 1927 exiled Kurds in such cities as Cairo, Paris, Beirut, and Damascus established a new Kurdish nationalist party, Hoyboun (meaning Independence). Hoyboun members created a base in northern Kurdistan and organized a fighting force to help liberate Turkish Kurds. Gaining the backing of Kurdish tribal leaders and civilians in the area, Hoyboun leaders declared their own government. Taking advantage of Turkey's slow response, Kurdish fighters seized control of territory from Mount Ararat down into southeastern Turkey. The Turkish government began to organize troops to quell the uprising.

This time, the Kurds were more organized and better prepared to fight the Turks. They were also receiving aid from Reza Khan in Iran, who wanted to weaken Turkey. In one month of fighting, the Kurds took 1,700 Turkish prisoners and captured a large amount of Turkish weaponry. Because of Mount Ararat's location on the border of Iran, Turkish troops could not surround the rebels. The rebel forces, on the other hand, were able to cross into Iranian territory and gather more supplies. But Iranian support ended when Turkish and Iranian leaders came to an agreement and renegotiated the border, with Iran getting land near Lake Van and with Turkey gaining territory around Mount Ararat.

The agreement enabled Turkish troops to surround Mount Ararat and the Kurdish forces. The Turkish troops then captured, killed, or drove the Kurds out of the area. For several more months, Turkish troops bombed and burned the Mount Ararat region, as well as other Kurdish territory, killing at least 3,000 children and adults, none of whom had been involved in the fighting. These killings were allowed under a new law, No. 1850, which protected the Turkish military from prosecution for killing the Kurds.

RESISTANCE TO ARAB RULE

Although less repressive, the situation for Kurds in Iraq was no more promising than it was in Turkey. In 1925 the League of Nations had sent a commission to Iraq to assess the situation in Mosul, where the Kurdish population was still resistant to Arab rule. Based on the findings of the commission, the League of Nations decided that Mosul should remain part of Iraq. The Kurds would not be independent but would be allowed to set up their own administration, to speak their own language, and to estab-

Because the British controlled the oil resources in Iraq, it was highly important to them that Mosul not be given over to the Kurds.

Independent Picture Service

lish their own schools and legal system. To further appease the Kurds, the Iraqi government established the Local Languages Law, which enabled the Kurds to learn Kurdish in primary schools in Sulaimaniyeh and Arbil, the main Kurdish regions. Although the Kurds did not gain the autonomy they had been promised, they accepted the arrangement.

By the end of the 1920s, Iraqis wanted to be free of British control. In 1929 British administrators met with leaders in Iraq to discuss the end of the British mandate. But the Iraqi Kurds were still concerned about what would happen to them once Iraq became free from British control. The British had pledged that the Iraqi government would abide by the provisions of the League of Nations mandate, but the Iraqis showed no signs of sticking to their previous promises. For example, the Iraqi government had made no effort to implement the Local Languages Law. Uneasy about their fate under an Arab government, Kurds staged strikes and demonstrations around Sulaimaniyeh and demanded independence.

Despite the objections of the Kurdish population, the British went ahead with their plans for Iraq. The Anglo-Iraqi Treaty ended the British mandate in 1932, and Iraq became formally independent. The Kurds rose again in revolt. It took three tries, but the Iraqi government eventually put down the Kurdish revolt with British air support. In the process, numerous Kurdish villages were destroyed.

Meanwhile, in Persia, Reza Khan was trying to disarm the Kurdish tribes and bring them under government control. But these goals proved difficult to achieve, especially since Kurdish leaders were constantly crossing the border from Iraq into Persia and stirring up feelings of Kurdish nationalism among tribes there. Another threat came from nomadic Kurdish tribes—such as the Kurdish Pizhdar—that lived in Qala Diza, Iraq, during the winter and migrated to Persia in the summer. Nomadic tribes like the Pizhdar made it more difficult to disarm and dissolve all tribes in Persia. To curb this annual influx of tribal members, Reza Khan imposed a poll tax on nomads.

Reza Khan also imposed

A Kurdish prisoner in Turkey. Determined to put an end to Kurdish nationalism, the Turkish government launched a massive wave of repression against the Kurdish population, during which thousands of Kurds were arrested, deported, and killed.

cultural restrictions on the population to make Persia a homogenous society. For instance, he made Persian the official and only language of the state, thus outlawing Kurdish, Turkish, Arabic, Baluchi and Luri. Khan also tried to create a uniform style of dress for all citizens of the country. This meant that the Kurds and other ethnic groups could no longer wear their traditional clothing.

Persian Kurdish tribes led a number of revolts in response to Reza Khan's attempts to disarm them and impose more restrictions on their culture. In response, Reza Khan's troops attacked and displaced Kurds from their tribal villages and encouraged tribal rivalry. Iranian forces executed a number of captured tribe-members and tribal chiefs and led air raids on Kurdish bases. Some tribal chiefs were forced to flee the country, while others were taken from their tribes and given land in another region of Iran. Kurdish tribalism in Iran wasn't eliminated, but it was severely disrupted and threatened. Some tribes fell into poverty as a result of this disruption and chaos.

During the same period, the Turkish government was creating new ways to handle its Kurdish population. Atatürk announced that only those of Turkish descent would have ethnic and national rights within the country and that any other ethnic groups would be stripped of their rights. He aimed to force minorities in Turkey to denounce their ethnic heritage, embrace and assimilate Turkish culture, or leave the country. Then, in 1932, the government established law No. 2510, which gave the government broad powers to move the population. The law divided Turkey into four zones that were to be repopulated. The purpose of the law was to eliminate Kurdish culture and identity by spreading out the Kurds so they didn't represent more than 5 percent of the population in any area. Over the next few years, Turkish soldiers forced hundreds of thousands of Kurds from their homes and marched them across the country. At the same time, the government granted land in Kurdistan to Turks.

In 1935 the Turkish government decided to subdue once and for all the Kurdish region of Dersim, which had managed to resist Turkish persecution and retain its autonomy. Dersim was in the zone that was to be completely evacuated under law No. 2510. From 1935 through 1938, the Turkish government put Dersim under a state of siege. Turkish forces bombed the Kurds and used poison gas against them. The Kurds were able to hold their ground for more than two years but eventually ran out of ammunition and were forced to flee. The assault on Dersim put an end to Kurdish political and military activity in Turkey for years to come.

In 1937 Turkey, Iran (which had officially changed its name from Persia in 1935), and Iraq signed the Saadabad Treaty. In this treaty, the three nations agreed to prevent "the formation and activity of associations, organizations, or armed bands seeking to overthrow established institutions." Although the agreement aimed to suppress any revolutionary movement, Kurdish separatism was a primary target. ⊕

CHAPTER
3
ENTRENCHED POSITIONS

Although most Middle Eastern countries weren't directly involved in World War II (1939–1945), the region was considered strategically important. The war forced the governments in Turkey, Iran, and Iraq to choose between fighting with the Allies (Britain, the United States, or with the Soviet Union) or with the Axis Powers (Germany, Italy, and Japan). Iran, in particular, had to deal with the Soviet Union's desire to acquire land in northern Iran. From this situation emerged the first real political movement by the Kurds.

THE MAHABAD REPUBLIC

In 1941 British and American forces overthrew Reza Khan, who they feared might have pro-Axis leanings. The Allies wanted control of Iran so that the British could ship supplies from the Persian Gulf to the Soviet Union via the Trans-Iranian Railway. They put Reza Khan's son, Mohammed Reza Pahlavi, into power in Tehran. The new shah signed a treaty allowing the British and the Soviets to use the railway and to keep troops in the country. The Soviets occupied the north of the country, where Kurdish and Azeri territories lay, while British and American forces occupied the rest of the country. The three powers agreed to withdraw from the country after the war.

Despite the presence of foreign troops, the government had very little control over much of the country. The weakness of the new Iranian government allowed the Kurds to organize. Around 1942 Iran's first major Kurdish political movement emerged when a group of Kurds from the town of Mahabad founded the Committee for the Revival of Kurdistan, known as Komala. Headed by educated, urban, middle-class intellectuals who supported Kurdish nationalism, the group gained support from Kurds in rural and urban areas of Iran. Komala chapters even formed in parts of Iraq and Turkey. Komala members wanted to obtain the right to use the Kurdish language in schools and government and to eliminate the intertribal conflicts that had been encouraged by Reza Khan.

A year after Komala was established, Mustafa Barzani, a Kurdish tribal leader, led a Kurdish revolt in Iraq. But with British help, the Iraqis drove Barzani and his 10,000 followers into Iranian Kurdistan, where they joined forces with Komala. From this combination emerged a new party called the Kurdistan Democratic Party of Iran (KDPI), established by Kurdish religious leader Qazi Mohammed in 1945. The KDPI issued a manifesto that listed eight points outlining the aspirations of the Kurdish people. The Kurds wanted the right to manage their own affairs and to obtain autonomy within Iran. They also wanted the right to study the Kurdish language and speak Kurdish in public. The manifesto demanded the right to improve the Kurds' economic state through the exploration of natural resources and the development of commerce within the region.

The Soviet Union strongly supported the KDPI. The Soviets wanted access to war materials that were carried from the Persian Gulf through Kurdish territory and up to the Soviet border. They didn't want to risk losing access to these supplies by angering Kurdish tribes. Therefore, they allowed the Kurds to govern themselves. The British and the Americans, on the other hand, didn't want to give the Kurds any self-governing power. They feared that if the Kurds gained autonomy,

Qazi Mohammed, a Kurdish religious leader, became the president of the Mahabad Republic in 1946.

other Iranian ethnic groups would rise up and demand the same freedoms.

In January 1946, with the encouragement of the Soviets, the KDPI took over the town of Mahabad and established the Mahabad Republic, the first Kurdish republic ever. KDPI delegates elected Qazi Mohammed as president and selected a parliament for the new republic, which would be defended by Mustafa Barzani and his men.

In the months that followed, Kurdish became the official language of the Mahabad Republic, several Kurdish magazines were established, and the economic situation improved dramatically. In addition, women were allowed to take part in government. The country also adopted a Kurdish flag. For the first time, it looked as if Kurdish unity might overcome tribal rivalry.

About a year after the Mahabad Republic was established and about six months after the end of World War II, however, tribal rivalries within the republic began heating up. Some of the Kurdish tribes felt oppressed by Barzani and his troops, while others distrusted the Soviet Union and resented Mohammed's reliance on Soviet support. Meanwhile, the British and the Americans had withdrawn their forces from the country and were pressuring the Soviets, who still had troops occupying parts of northern Iran, to do so as well. The Soviets pulled their forces out of northern Iran after signing an agreement with Iran to form a joint Irano-Soviet oil company. This agreement immediately ended Soviet support of the Kurds and enabled the Iranian government to reestablish its control over the country.

Without Soviet support, Qazi Mohammed realized that the Mahabad Republic would be unable to put up a fight against the U.S.- and British-backed Iranian government, which had no intentions of allowing Kurdish autonomy. Hoping to salvage some freedom for the Kurds of Mahabad, Mohammed went to Tehran to ask the Iranian leadership for Kurdish autonomy within Iran, but he was denied. After Mohammed and the Mahabad parliament pledged armed resistance, the Iranian government sent troops to destroy the Kurdish republic. Mohammed surrendered and was arrested, but Barzani and his forces escaped. A year later, the Iranian government hung Mohammed and other KDPI leaders in public and conducted mass executions throughout Iranian Kurdistan. All traces of the Mahabad Republic were erased.

The KDPI continued its activities after the fall of the republic, but most of its members went underground and focused their efforts on the Kurdish movement in Iraq, where Mustafa Barzani and a group of Kurdish intellectuals formed the Kurdish Democratic Party (KDP), an Iraqi version of the KDPI. The Iranian government continued to suppress Kurdish nationalism, and Iranian forces moved to crush the last remnants of Kurdish autonomy. Iranian troops killed thousands of Kurds, drove others from their homes, and flattened hundreds of villages.

REFORM AND REVOLUTION
While the Iranian government was cracking down on the Kurds, the Turkish government was beginning to ease its repression of the Kurdish population. To gain financial and military support from Britain and the United

In use since 1944, this flag represents Kurds in Iran and Iraq.

A Kurdish family in Iraq during the 1950s. Because much of Iraqi Kurdistan was undeveloped, many Kurdish peasants lived in poverty.

States, the Turkish government decided it needed to become more democratic and less repressive. So in 1950 Turkey held its first free elections, which resulted in a victory for the Democratic Party. This victory brought new hope for Turkish Kurds after the repression and forced displacement that had occurred under Atatürk. Kurdish politicians gained some seats in the Turkish parliament, and the Kurdish provinces of southeastern Turkey—which were impoverished due to government neglect—began to see some economic improvements. Exiled Kurdish leaders were allowed back into the country. New laws enabled Kurds to speak Kurdish, although only in private.

Despite these advances, however, the Turkish government still did not recognize the Kurds as a separate group of people. In fact, Kurdish politicians could only serve in parliament if they forgot that they were Kurds. When Kurdish intellectuals in Turkey began publishing a daily paper that discussed the underdevelopment of southeastern Turkey, Turkish president Adnan Menderes had the paper closed and the publishers arrested.

The next major event to affect the Kurds was the Iraqi Revolution of 1958, in which Iraqi general Abdul Karim Qasim and a group called the Free Officers overthrew the monarchy in Iraq and declared a republic. As the new Iraqi leader, Qasim made several reforms that benefited the Iraqi Kurds. For example, he drew up a new constitution that recognized Kurdish as an official language (along with Arabic), and he legalized the publication of about 14 different Kurdish journals. Qasim also invited Mustafa Barzani, the acknowledged leader of the Kurdish nationalist movement, back into the country. Qasim even appointed Barzani as the chairman of the KDP.

Qasim's popularity among Iraqi Kurds didn't last long, however. Qasim had hoped to control Barzani and use him as an ally against the enemies of the government, including some rebellious Kurdish groups. But Barzani was a popular figure among many Iraqi Kurds, and his power became a threat to the Iraqi president. As a result, in 1960 Qasim banned all Kurdish publications and political parties, including the KDP, and established a military dictatorship. While trying to pit the Kurdish tribal groups against one another, he also limited the amount of land the Kurds could have and established new taxes. When the Kurds asked for autonomy, Qasim refused. Qasim's new policies aimed to unify the country's Arabs and stifle its Kurdish population.

Qasim's change of heart led the Iraqi Kurds to launch a rebellion in 1961. Originally a tribal revolt against Qasim's land reforms, the rebellion eventually grew into a Kurdish liberation movement led by KDP members Mustafa Barzani, Ibrahim Ahmad, and Jalal Talabani. The movement attracted people of all classes in Iraqi Kurdish society, from peasants and farmers to the educated elites. Once the liberation movement was under way, the Iraqi Kurds organized a Revolutionary Command Council. They set up political, civil, and judicial systems and organized

Mustafa Barzani (far left) *meets with Kurdish fighters at a mountain hideout in northern Iraq. Although outnumbered by the Iraqi army, the Kurdish peshmergas, skilled in mountain fighting, were able to hold their own.*

AP/Wide World Photos

public health, education, foreign affairs, defense, and national security offices. The Kurdish Revolutionary Army—whose members were called *peshmergas*—was established by Barzani to unite Kurdish forces and end tribal rivalry.

From 1961 to 1963, the Iraqi Kurds fought numerous battles against Iraqi forces. Then, in 1963, members of the Baath Party—an Iraqi socialist political party—assassinated President Qasim and took control of the government. The Kurds had allied themselves with the Baath Party in return for the promise of autonomy, and after the coup the two groups declared a cease-fire. Barzani demanded recognition of Kurdish autonomy and requested that the Kurds be allowed to collect oil revenue proportional to the Kurdish population of Iraq. But the new government refused the Kurdish demands for autonomy because, as one report said, it wouldn't have made sense for Iraq to give such a large and rich land area to such a small population. In addition, if the Iraqi government were to give the Kurds this land, the Iraqi economy would suffer. The government also objected to the Kurds' request to legally form their own army, which was deemed unnecessary. The Baath Party had no more intention of granting the Kurds' self-rule than had Qasim.

After refuting Barzani's demands, the Iraqi government launched a new offensive against the Kurds. At the same time, the Baath Party also began its Arabization program, forcing Kurds out of their homes and villages and replacing them with Arab citizens. Later, in 1963, Iraqi president Abdul Salam Aref removed all Baathists from his government, but he continued the war against the Kurds.

As the war against the Iraqi government dragged on, a large divide grew within the KDP. Barzani disagreed with Ibrahim Ahmad and Jalal Talabani about the goals of the Kurdish movement and how to deal with the Iraqi government. While Barzani was willing to accept Iraqi recognition of the Kurds as a separate and distinct group, Ahmad and Talabani wanted complete autonomy for the Kurds. Barzani and his supporters sought total control of the KDP. The friction between the KDP leaders caused rifts within the liberation movement. In 1964, following more fighting among the KDP leaders, Barzani managed to oust Ahmad and Talabani from the KDP and take full control of the group.

SHIFTING POSITIONS

During the uprising in Iraq, Turkish Kurds were seeing more signs of reform. In 1961 a new Turkish government, under the leadership of Cemal Gursel, adopted a new constitution that gave citizens several democratic rights, including freedom of the press, the right to form independent trade unions and associations, and the right to strike and attend public meetings. The Kurds were directly affected by these reforms. Kurdish authors began writing about Kurdish culture and history in newly established magazines and newspapers such as *Baris Dunyasi* (World of Peace), a journal that dealt with Kurdish literature, language, and folklore. Kurds also joined several new political parties that had formed, including the New Turkey Party, the Turkish Workers Party, and the Justice Party. But the Turkish government still denied the existence of Kurdish identity and responded harshly to any attempts to express that identity.

By the mid-1960s, Turkish government officials had become concerned about the Kurdish uprising in Iraq and the effect it was having on Turkish Kurds. As a result, they cracked down on expressions of Kurdish identity. In 1966 the Turkish government began banning Kurdish journals because Turkish officials believed they were helping rekindle Kurdish nationalism. The government also arrested editors of Kurdish journals. Fearing that the Kurdish uprising in Iraq would stir feelings of nationalism among Turkish Kurds, the government then set up commando groups to police Kurdish villages and to prevent peasants from forming revolutionary groups. The commando groups scoured the Kurdish regions, torturing, raping, and hanging Kurds.

Rather than suppressing Kurdish nationalism, these

Betrayal by Iraqi Kurds

The Kurdish revolt in Iraq provides an example of how Kurdish groups have betrayed one another, and how the governments of the region have played a role in the betrayals. In a show of solidarity, the Iranian Kurds fully supported the Kurdish liberation movement in Iraq. KDPI fighters joined in the struggle against the Iraqi government and supplied weapons for the cause. Between 1961 and 1966, this assistance helped the Iraqi Kurds survive against the larger and more powerful Iraqi army. The KDPI hoped that Kurdish success in Iraq would help their own fight against the repressive regime of the Iranian shah.

This support was soon undercut by the shah, who began supporting Barzani in hopes he would weaken the Iraqi government. But the shah also wanted Barzani and the KDP to become dependent upon his aid. He hoped that Barzani and the KDP could help curb Kurdish uprisings in Iran. The shah's plan worked, and Barzani and the KDP became dependent upon his aid. In order to ensure that they continued to receive aid for their war against the Iraqi government, Barzani and the KDP leadership urged the KDPI to freeze its activities. This betrayal caused the Iranian Kurds to launch an 18-month attack against the Tehran government, a revolt that was crushed by 1968 with the help of the KDP leadership.

tactics only encouraged the Kurdish opposition. Kurds responded by forming nationalist groups and staging large protests in Kurdish cities throughout southeastern Turkey. These acts marked the beginning of a shift in the Kurdish struggle in Turkey. Kurdish activists realized that an organized, political campaign for Kurdish rights might be more

successful than a military campaign. Nonetheless, the Turkish government still responded to Kurdish political activity with a heavy hand. The Turks began clamping down on Kurdish revolutionary movements, killing activists at universities and banning student, teacher, and youth organizations. The Turkish government also continued to strip away Kurdish freedoms. Troops began to arrest Kurds regularly on charges that they were supporting Barzani in Iraq or were involved with another Kurdish group that had formed in Turkey.

Meanwhile, in Iraq, the fighting between the Iraqi government and the Kurds continued until 1966, when a new cease-fire was declared and the Iraqi prime minister began negotiating with Barzani. These talks resulted in the Declaration of June 29, which recognized the "binational character of the Iraqi state." The declaration meant that the Iraqi government would acknowledge Arabs and Kurds as equal partners. In 1968, however, the Baath Party overthrew the Iraqi president in another military coup. The new Iraqi president, Ahmad Hassan al-Bakr, and his vice president, Saddam Hussein, ended all talks with the Kurds. In April 1969, the Iraqis launched their fourth war against the Kurds, slaughtering and displacing Kurds in Arbil and Kirkuk.

THE MARCH 11 AGREEMENT
In 1970, after two more years of fighting, the Iraqi government and the KDP signed the March 11 Agreement, a deal that nearly earned the Iraqi Kurds their long-sought freedom. In this agreement, negotiated between Vice President Hussein and Mustafa Barzani, the Iraqi government promised the Kurds autonomy, hoping to end the ongoing fighting.

The March 11 Agreement divided the Iraqi Republic into 16 counties or provinces, called *muhafazats*. Three of the muhafazats—including Arbil, Dohuk, and Sulaimaniyeh—were located in the Kurdish autonomous region. The agreement contained 15 articles that called for an autonomous Kurdistan, a Kurdish university, Kurdish cultural rights, the

As vice president, Saddam Hussein played a significant role in the Iraqi government's war against the Kurds.

right to free speech, the right to establish a Kurdish TV station, and the freedom to teach in the Kurdish language. Both sides saw the agreement as an historic event. In an act of goodwill, the Kurds dissolved their Revolutionary Command Council, as well as the administrative offices they had set up in 1964. The Iraqi government moved several Kurds into governmental positions.

But the agreement immediately ran into difficulties. As part of the deal, the Iraqi government had agreed to conduct a census by March 11, 1971, to determine where the majority of Iraqi Kurds lived. This area would become the Kurdish autonomous region. The government claimed Kurdistan would achieve full autonomy by March 11, 1974, at the latest. The KDP, knowing that many Kurds had been forced to relocate since the early 1960s, asked the government to consider this population shift when taking the census. The Kurdish requests, however, fell on deaf ears. The Iraqi government knew that the oil-rich region of Kirkuk was mostly Kurd-

The Iraqi government knew that the oil-rich region of Kirkuk was mostly Kurdish but didn't want to lose this territory, so they continually delayed taking the census and instead embarked on a mission of Arabization.

ish but didn't want to lose this territory, so they continually delayed taking the census and embarked instead on a mission of Arabization. During Baghdad's renewed Arabization process, the Iraqi government moved Kurds from Mosul and Kirkuk and replaced them with Arab citizens.

The Kurds complained that the Arabization project violated an article of the agreement that had called for an end to the Arabization of Kurdistan. They demanded that the government repatriate (return) Kurds and Arabs to their original areas and insisted that Kirkuk be included in the autonomous

A peshmerga overlooks a mountain pass in northern Iraq. While Mustafa Barzani negotiated with the Iraqi government, fighting between the two sides continued throughout the early 1970s.

region. But the Iraqi government claimed that the Kurds had also broken a number of the articles in the agreement and that Barzani was not being cooperative. According to the Iraqi government, Barzani said he wouldn't acknowledge the census if it showed that any of the Kurdish regions had an Arab majority. The government also objected to Barzani's insistence that the Kurdish region receive a proportional distribution of oil revenue. Iraqi leaders believed that if they gave Barzani and the Kurds too much land and power, the Kurds would try to break away from Iraq and claim independence.

As the Iraqi government expelled Kurds from their homes, Hussein tried to provoke the Kurds into fighting. The Iraqi secret service made two attempts to assassinate Barzani and repeatedly tried to divide the KDP. In addition, the Iraqi government continued to discriminate against the Kurds economically, culturally, and politically. Many Kurdish children were unable to get school grants for or admittance into schools and universities. In the Kurdish regions, the government made few economic plans for development. And the Kurds who had been given positions in the Iraqi government found that they had no decision-making power.

THE 1974–75 WAR

Baghdad established the Autonomous Region of Kurdistan on March 11, 1974, despite Kurdish protests over the fact that Kirkuk was not included. To sway Kurdish opinion, the Iraqi government began to recognize Kurdish national rights and allow children in the autonomous region to study Kurdish. The Baghdad government also agreed to set up a legislative assembly and an executive council for the Kurds.

Iraq gave the KDP two weeks to accept the agreement. Barzani was clearly not satisfied with the new political structure, since it gave the Kurds fewer rights and less territory than they wanted. In addition, Barzani felt that, with Iranian support, Kurdish forces could hold their own against the Iraqi army. Barzani and the KDP rejected the autonomy deal, and war between the Kurds and Iraq broke out once again. Despite receiving military aid from Iran and greater support from Kurdish citizens, the Kurdish fighters didn't have enough weapons to battle Iraq and win.

The rights Iraq had given to the Kurds were soon revoked. After launching the offensive against Barzani and his troops, the Iraqi government eliminated Kurdish school programs, banned the Kurdish language, and rewrote schoolbooks to eliminate any references to the Kurds.

Iraq's Arabization program came back in full force, as Iraqi soldiers forced as many as a million Kurds from their homes and replaced them with Arab citizens. The government sent many of the displaced Kurds to resettlement camps. In other instances, Iraqi troops split up Kurdish families and moved them to villages in southern Iraq or housing projects in Baghdad. These new living arrangements clashed with the clan and tribal lifestyles of the Iraqi Kurds. The Iraqi government claimed the moves were necessary, in order to distribute laborers around the region and to provide proper security along the frontiers.

In early 1975, the autonomy agreement officially collapsed, and the Iraqi government reestablished its borders so that more Kurdish land, especially the oil-rich area around Kirkuk, could be populated with Arabs. Iraqi soldiers expelled hundreds of Kurdish families from their homes in Kirkuk and Kifri, then bulldozed the dwellings and poisoned the water sources. Soon afterward, the Iraqi government shut down the Kurdish daily newspaper, banned all political organizations, and gave Barzani an ultimatum—accept a new agreement that didn't guarantee Kurdish rights or fight. Barzani rejected the plan, opting to continue the war.

Despite significant victories by the Iraqi army, Barzani kept fighting. The shah of Iran, wanting the war to drag on and weaken the Iraqi government, continued to support the Kurds. But by this time, Iran's support of the Kurds had heightened tensions between the two nations. To avoid a war between Iran and Iraq, other Arab leaders tried to diffuse the situation. Their efforts

Negotiations between the shah of Iran (center) *and Saddam Hussein* (right) *led to the end of Iranian support for the Iraqi Kurds. Without Iranian support, the Kurds were routed by Iraqi forces.*

resulted in the Algiers Agreement, signed in March 1975. In this treaty, the shah of Iran agreed to secure the border between Iran and Iraqi Kurdistan and stop supplying the Kurds with aid. In return, the shah received some territorial concessions from Iraq.

In a meeting with Barzani, the shah told the Kurdish leader that he and his men could continue fighting with a closed frontier, seek refuge in Iran, or surrender to the Iraqis. The next day, however, the Iranian forces stopped supporting the Kurds. Iraqi troops attacked Kurdish forces and villages, killing, capturing, and displacing thousands. After a short period of fighting, Barzani surrendered and retreated to Iran with other KDP leaders. Iraq's renewed offensive also caused a massive Kurdish exodus, as hundreds of thousands of Kurdish civilians escaped to Iran with Barzani and his forces.

Barzani's retreat effectively ended the war, but the Kurdish battle for freedom endured. Political groups run by Kurdish students and militants started popping up in Iraq. Jalal Talabani also reappeared, as head of the Patriotic Union of Kurdistan (PUK). The KDP eventually reestablished friendly relations with Iran, while the PUK sought support from Syria. In March 1976, Mustafa Barzani left Iran and went to the United States to receive medical treatment for lung cancer. His sons, Idris and Massoud, took over leadership of the KDP. Meanwhile, the Iraqi government continued to remove people from the Kurdish Autonomous Region.

The Kurdish movement in Turkey was heating up as well. During the 1970s, Turkish leaders tried to stamp out all manifestations of Kurdish nationalism, but Kurdish activists continued to pursue their political campaign for freedom and economic improvements. Throughout the impoverished Kurdish provinces of southeastern Turkey, Kurdish political groups held meetings and organized demonstrations. They hoped to increase Kurdish national consciousness and make the Turkish public more aware of

Soviet and U.S. Support

In the 1970s, the Middle East was one of the regional battlegrounds in the cold war between the United States and the Soviet Union. Seeking allies in the Middle East, both countries became involved in the conflict between Iraq and its Kurdish population. In 1972 the Soviets began supporting the Baathist government of Iraq. The two countries signed the Treaty of Friendship and Cooperation, which called for the Soviets to supply the Iraqis with weapons. Iraq would allow the Soviet navy access to its ports. The United States, meanwhile, became friendly with Iran. After U.S. president Richard Nixon's visit to Iran in 1972, the United States donated $16 million in aid to the Kurds. The aid was authorized by President Nixon and Henry Kissinger, who would become secretary of state.

But the aid to the Kurds was not a sign of U.S. support for Kurdish nationalism. When Nixon resigned from the presidency in 1974, the American government organized a committee to analyze the financial dealings made during Nixon's term. The Pike House Committee Report, released in 1976, outlined what the committee believed were the real reasons why the U.S. and Iranian governments had agreed to support the Kurds. As it turned out, neither government actually wanted the Kurds to beat the Iraqis. According to the report, "Neither the foreign head of state (the shah) nor the president and Dr. Kissinger desired victory for our clients (the Kurds). They merely hoped to ensure that the insurgents would be capable of sustaining a level of hostility just high enough to sap the resources of the neighboring state (Iraq)." One of the reasons cited in the Pike report was that the United States didn't want to see Iraq gain too much power.

the government's repression.

The Kurdish movement was just one element of an increasingly violent political struggle in Turkey between left-wing and right-wing political groups, which were battling over the direction of the country. The left-wing groups—which supported Kurdish rights—wanted a more democratic government. The right-wing organizations—which opposed Kurdish rights—felt that Turkey was straying too far from the nationalist policies of Atatürk. The heart of this conflict was in Turkish Kurdistan. In 1978, after clashes between left-wing and right-wing groups in southeastern Turkey caused a number of deaths, the Turkish government established martial (military) law in the 13 provinces that made up Turkish Kurdistan. Turkish troops were sent to the region to quell the fighting. Although the move was intended to stop the violence, it also aimed to suppress Kurdish nationalism in the region.

This new wave of repression pushed Kurdish university student Abdullah Ocalan to establish the Partia Karkaren Kurdistan, or Kurdish Workers Party. Unlike the Kurdish groups in Iran and Iraq, the PKK claimed its goal was to fight for all Kurds, rather than just Kurds in Turkey.

REVOLUTION IN IRAN

The next significant Kurdish uprising occurred in Iran. While the shah of Iran was supporting the efforts of the Iraqi Kurds in order to destabilize the Iraqi government, he was also suppressing his own Kurdish population. To centralize his authority over the Iranian people, the shah eliminated all political groups, professional organizations, and non-Shiite religious groups. He denied freedom of the press and even began to control people's movements between villages. The shah suppressed all demands for national rights from Iranian minority groups.

In the late 1970s, the Iranian government launched an aggressive economic growth plan for the state. The plan backfired, however, and

After the Iranian Revolution, the Ayatollah Khomeini (above) became the new leader of Iran. But KDPI head Abdul Rahman Ghassemlou (facing page, top) found the new Iranian leader was also opposed to Kurdish autonomy.

prices and inflation soared. The dismal economy and the government's oppressive tactics led to widespread social unrest among the rising number of Iranians who opposed the shah. In January 1979, the shah left the country, leaving his prime minister in charge. Once again, Iranian Kurds tried to take advantage

The Kurdish Library

The Kurds hoped that the new Iranian government might be more sympathetic to their desire for autonomy. But Khomeini, who had abolished the monarchy and had established an Islamic republic in Iran, wasn't interested in giving the Kurds autonomy either. His forces—the Revolutionary Guard—were battling the Kurdish fighters. Khomeini, who was Shiite, declared the war against the mostly Sunni Kurds a holy war, claiming the Kurds were trying to undermine Islam. Iranian forces tried to crush the Kurdish uprisings by bombing Kurd- ish towns, destroying villages, and killing hundreds of Kurds. Khomeini had Kurdish leaders arrested and executed after quick trials. He soon took over all Iranian Kurdish towns and put them under military control. But Kurdish fighters still controlled much of the countryside.

Finally, in November 1979, the Iranian government and the Kurds declared a ceasefire. One month later, representatives of the Iranian government traveled to Mahabad to negotiate with the Kurds. To discourage the Kurds and other minorities of the country's political instability to obtain autonomy. The KDPI, led by Abdul Rahman Ghassemlou, organized uprisings in Iran's Kurdish regions and captured much of Iranian Kurdistan from Iranian forces. In February of that year, the Ayatollah Khomeini, leader of the country's Islamic fundamentalists, overthrew the shah's government. In March the KDPI, which had been operating secretly for about 30 years, met in Mahabad and declared itself a legal political group.

UPI/Corbis-Bettmann

To crush the Kurdish uprising, Khomeini had a number of Kurdish leaders executed.

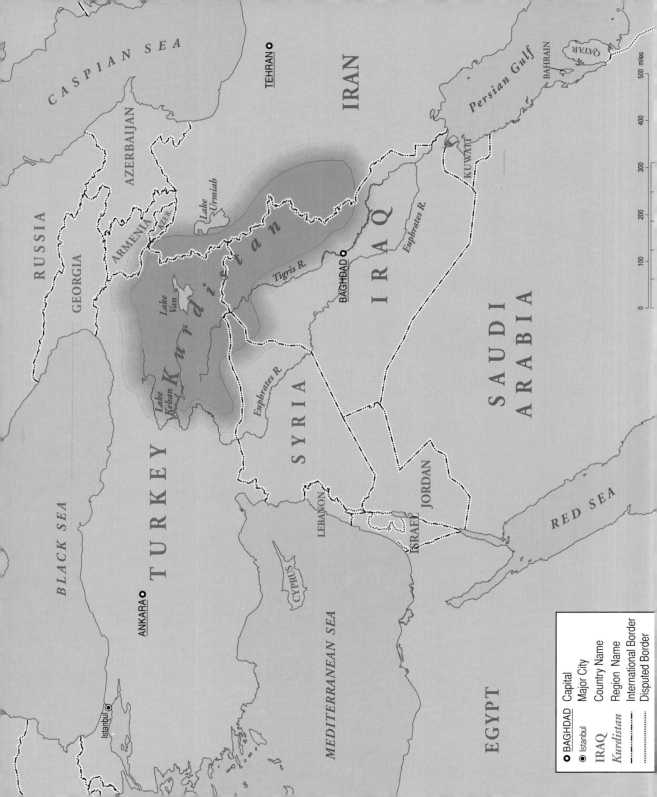

Facing page: *In 1980 the long-standing Iran-Iraq rivalry turned into all-out war. The conflict was sparked by boundary disputes between the two nations, but Iran's support for Iraq's Kurdish and Shiite populations also played a role.*

from leading uprisings, the government delegation offered a new arrangement for Iranian minorities. But their offer did not include Kurdish autonomy, and fighting resumed. In 1980 Iran's new president, Abolhassan Bani-Sadr, refused an autonomy plan put forward by Qassemlou and began to use more force to suppress the Kurds.

IRAN-IRAQ WAR

In 1980 the Kurds in Iran and Iraq became tangled in a larger conflict between their respective states when the long-simmering tension between Iran and Iraq boiled over into armed conflict. The conflict began when Iraqi president Saddam Hussein (who had taken office in 1979) demanded a revision of the Algiers Agreement, which Iran subsequently re-

jected. On September 22, 1980, Iraq invaded Iran, beginning an eight-year war.

The Iran-Iraq War provided the Kurds in both countries with the opportunity to revive their struggle for autonomy and possibly independence. But Kurdish efforts were repeatedly hampered by the inability of the different factions to work together. Instead of uniting for the common Kurdish cause, each Kurdish faction in Iran and Iraq pursued the alliance that helped them the most. As a result, the KDP sought Iran's support in its war against Hussein, while the KDPI looked to Iraq to help fight the government of Iran. In addition, the KDP and PUK fought with one another over differing tactics in the struggle for Kurdish independence in Iraq. This led to a deal between PUK leader Talabani and Hussein, in which the PUK agreed to aid the Iraqi forces fighting the KDP. In other words, the Kurds ended up fighting against each other.

The inability of the Kurds to establish a united front during the Iran-Iraq War enabled the Iraqi and Iranian forces, which had reached a

stalemate with one another, to respond to the two Kurdish insurgencies. Iran, with the help of the KDP, was able to subdue the KDPI and reestablish control of Iranian Kurdistan. With the aid of the PUK, Hussein launched an offensive to wipe out the KDP. Then, after breaking ties with the PUK in 1984, Hussein sent troops to wipe out areas occupied by PUK fighters.

As the Iran-Iraq War dragged on, the Iraqis continued to assault the Kurds, destroying villages, expelling people from homes, closing schools, and denying people social and health services. The devastation caused by the Iraqi offensive brought the Iraqi Kurds together. In 1987 six Kurdish parties—including the KDP, the PUK, the Socialist Party of Kurdistan, the Kurdistan Democratic Party, the Kurdish Socialist Party, and the Iraqi Communist Party—established the Kurdistan Front. The front's main goal was to obtain Kurdish national rights within Iraq, but it also aimed to overthrow Hussein and establish a democratic government in Iraq. Hoping that the Kurdistan Front could

Iraq's chemical attacks against the Kurds destroyed Kurdish villages and killed at least 100,000 Kurdish civilians. The Iraqi government claimed that Iran was responsible for the chemical attacks.

help them break the stalemate and win the war, the Iranians allowed the front to set up military bases near the Iran-Iraq border. Soon the Iranians and Kurdistan Front forces were able to advance into Iraq and close in on Suleimaniyeh. The tide of the war appeared to be turning in favor of Iran.

The Iraqi government, losing ground, opted for new fighting tactics, including the use of chemical and biological weapons. These new tactics brought the Kurdish struggle into the international spotlight. Beginning in 1987, Iraqi forces launched a series of devastating chemi-

cal attacks—in which Iraqi jets dropped bombs containing mustard gas, nerve gas, and the disease anthrax—on the Kurds. Known as Operation Anfal, these attacks killed thousands of Kurds and destroyed Kurdish towns, farms, crops, and livestock. Estimates claim that the Iraqis destroyed between 4,000 and 4,500 Kurdish villages and forced 500,000 to 1.5 million people into refugee camps. After the attacks, as many as 182,000 Kurds were missing. The Iraqi forces also used chemical weapons against Iranian troops. After these attacks, the Iranians, who were low

on supplies and defenseless against chemical weapons, began to lose the war against Iraq. On August 16, 1988, the Iranians agreed to a cease-fire.

Following the cease-fire, the Iraqis turned their full attention to the Kurds. Those who had stayed in Iraq became the victims of more chemical attacks. During the last phase of Operation Anfal, the Iraqi air force dropped chemical weapons on Badinan to wipe out the entire Kurdish population in Northern Iraq. Thousands of men, women, and children— mainly civilians—were killed, and thousands were captured. Iraqi forces tortured, jailed, and executed Kurdish fighters and civilians. The KDP and the PUK were dealt a severe blow.

After the war, about 100,000 Iraqi Kurds fled to Turkey, fearing that Hussein

Iraq's Chemical Attacks against the Kurds

Although Saddam Hussein had used chemical weapons in the Iran-Iraq War as early as 1983, the first of a series of attacks featuring chemical and biological weapons began in 1987, when Iraqi planes bombed Kurdish civilians and peshmergas in Sulaimaniyeh province. By mid-1987, chemical and biological weapons were being used against the Kurds on a regular basis. Mustard gas was the most commonly used chemical weapon.

In 1988, between February and October, Hussein began Operation Anfal, during which the Kurds were repeatedly bombarded with chemical agents. The Iraqis led massive air raids against the Kurds and then followed these with ground attacks on Kurdish villages, towns, and agricultural fields. It is believed that at least 100,000 civilians were killed during Operation Anfal. Due to Iraq's strict laws against freedom of the press, however, most Kurds didn't know about this disaster until 1991, when Kurds took photos from village to village to show people what had happened. It's believed that many Kurds were also shielded from news of this event because they had escaped to the mountains and did not have access to information.

The most notorious chemical attack against the Kurds took place March 16, 1988, in Halabja, an Iraqi Kurdish town about 15 miles from the Iran-Iraq border. On that day, Iraqi planes dropped bombs that were filled with mustard gas, cyanide (a poison), and nerve gas. Kurdish civilians were poisoned, asphyxiated, burned, and blown apart by the air attack. The streets of Halabja were scattered with the bodies of men, women, and children of all ages. Nearly 5,000 people died.

Human rights groups consider the Halabja attack an act of genocide. The Iraqi government said its attack on Halabja was justified because the town had been overthrown by Iranian and Kurdish forces 48 hours earlier. Some believe the peshmergas were at fault for instigating the Iraqi-led attack, since they had captured this civilian town for the Iranians and knew the Iraqis might retaliate and try to reclaim it.

would continue to launch chemical attacks against them. The exiled Kurds—who had no shelter or protection from the winter weather—created a refugee problem in Turkey. At one point, up to a dozen people were dying each day, while as many as 350 people died in one week. The Turkish government feared these refugees would link up with Kurdish militants in southeastern Turkey. To persuade the refugees to leave, Turkey made them live in camps and provided little aid for them.

EMERGENCE OF THE PKK

While the Iran-Iraq War was dragging on, Turkey was also experiencing upheaval. In 1980 Turkish military leaders, who had grown tired of the government's inability to stifle conflicts between left- and right-wing groups, overthrew the government in a bloodless coup. In 1981 the new military leaders banned political parties and reestablished martial law throughout the Kurdish region. Turkish troops began patrolling the streets and border regions of southeastern Turkey, arresting and torturing Kurds suspected of political activity.

But the government's repression only encouraged Kurdish nationalism. Protests against the government's harsh tactics continued, helping to foster a sense of Kurdish national identity. During the crackdown, PKK leader Abdullah Ocalan, the main target of the new government, escaped to Syria and began organizing a guerrilla force with other Kurds living there. Syria supplied the Kurds with weapons, money, uniforms, and training in guerrilla warfare, in the hope of destabilizing the Turkish government.

In 1983 Turkey returned to civilian rule when Turkish citizens elected a new government to be led by President Evran Kenan and Prime Minister Turgut Ozal. But the new government maintained martial law and continued its Kurdish policies, which included the mass arrest and execution of Kurdish activists and the forced relocation of Kurdish civilians. In 1983 Turkey again prohibited use of the Kurdish language by constitutional law. The government also neglected the administrative and economic needs of the Kurdish provinces. Amid the discontent of Kurdish civilians in southeastern Turkey, the PKK began a major military campaign against the Turkish government. The PKK hoped to completely drive Turkish forces from southeastern Turkey and to reduce the government's control over the region.

The influx of Kurdish refugees from Iraq added to Turkey's growing Kurdish dilemma. Although not the only group fighting for Kurdish rights in Turkey, the PKK became the focus of Turkish concerns. Since starting their guerrilla war, PKK fighters had stepped up their attacks against Turkish security

Abdullah Ocalan greets PKK guerrillas training in Lebanon. After fleeing Turkey, Ocalan planned and organized PKK activities from Syria.

© M. Attar/Sygma

forces and Kurdish landlords, whom they believed were oppressing the Kurdish peasantry and aiding the government. These attacks brought the Kurdish issue into the national spotlight and made it appear that the government had no control over Turkey's southeastern provinces.

The Turkish government declared war on the Kurdish insurgency. In 1987 the government placed a governor-general in charge of the eight Kurdish provinces, which were already under martial law. The governor-general was responsible for coordinating the efforts of Turkish security forces, which included security sweeps meant to root out PKK guerillas and collaborators. These security sweeps led to mass arrests and torture of Kurdish civilians. Decree 285, introduced in 1988, gave the governor-general the power to evacuate villages and deport the population. To further defend against PKK activity and to prevent the organization from gaining further support, the government also began to arm Kurdish villagers. These village guards, whom the government armed and paid a regular salary, became a militia force that assisted the Turkish army and local police forces.

The village guard system presented a new dilemma for Kurdish civilians in southeastern Turkey. Kurds who chose not to become village guards were beaten or killed by Turkish soldiers. But the PKK also dealt harshly with village guards and any Kurds suspected of collaborating with the government. Over a period of two years, PKK fighters launched a vicious assault on the village guard system, killing many guards and their families. In addition, PKK fighters demanded support—often with force—from Kurds in villages around the region. Village leaders were required to give food, money, weapons, and other supplies to the cause. Many Kurds criticized the PKK for using such extreme tactics, which eventually caused a rift with other Kurdish factions outside of Turkey. Yet despite this opposition, the PKK began to gain a large and loyal following among impoverished Kurds in southeastern Turkey.

The Turkish government took other approaches to curb the growth of Kurdish nationalism. In April 1990, the government passed Decree 213, which gave the governor-general the power to close any publishing house that "falsely reflects events in the region or engages in untruthful reporting or commentary." This law essentially censored any reporting of the conflict between the government and the PKK, thereby preventing Turkish citizens from learning about what was going on in southeastern Turkey.

By the end of the 1980s, the Kurds were fighting separate wars on various fronts. In Turkey the PKK's battle against the Turkish government was growing increasingly violent. Meanwhile, in Iraq, Saddam Hussein continued his efforts to destroy the Kurdistan Front. In Iran the Kurdish movement was dealt a blow when KDPI leader Abdul Rahman Qassemlou was assassinated in Vienna, Austria. Qassemlou had gone to Vienna for secret negotiation with representatives of the Iranian government. The two parties were meeting to discuss a solution to the Kurdish problem in Iran. ⊕

CHAPTER

4

THE PRESENT CONFLICT

On August 2, 1990, Saddam Hussein ordered Iraqi forces to invade and seize control of Kuwait—a tiny Arab nation wedged between Iraq, Saudi Arabia, and the Persian Gulf. Hussein's aim was to annex the oil-rich country for its resources and to gain access to the large Kuwaiti port on the Persian Gulf. He hoped that by gaining control of Kuwait, Iraq would become stronger and wealthier. To justify the invasion, Hussein claimed that Kuwait had been illegally tapping oil from the Ar Rumaylah oil field, which sits on the Iraq-Kuwait border and is shared by both countries.

The United Nations (UN) condemned the invasion and imposed economic **sanctions** on Iraq to force Hussein to remove his troops. On January 17, 1991, after UN Security Council sanctions and ultimatums failed to deter

Hussein, a **coalition** force led by the United States launched air strikes against Iraqi troops in Kuwait and on targets in Iraq. In what became known as the Gulf War, the United States and its allies bombed Iraqi troops in Kuwait to force them out of the region and attacked sites around Iraq to weaken Hussein's military power and to deplete his country's resources. After about six weeks of fighting, the coalition forces liberated Kuwait and the Gulf War officially ended.

During the crisis in Kuwait, the Kurdistan Front began a new effort to overthrow Hussein. With encouragement and support from Iran, Saudi Arabia, Syria, Britain, and the United States, the Front tried to unite all parties opposed to the Iraqi government. At a January meeting in Saudi Arabia, 20 Iraqi op-

position parties signed a statement that condemned Iraq's invasion of Kuwait and promised to put an end to Hussein's rule. In March the uprisings began. Shiite Muslims revolted in southern Iraq, and the Kurds rebelled in northern Iraq. With the majority of Iraqi forces in Kuwait, Kurdish peshmergas easily captured the cities of Kirkuk, Sulaimaniyeh, Arbil, and Dohuk. Hussein's regime appeared to be crumbling.

But the Iraqi government didn't fall as the coalition forces had hoped. Battered but not defeated, Hussein was able to remain in control. After his troops were defeated in the Gulf War, Hussein sent what was left of the Republican Guard—his elite military forces—to crush the revolts in northern and southern Iraq. The war had left the Iraqi economy in shambles. Due to the

Iraq's invasion of Kuwait led to a massive bombing campaign against Iraq by coalition forces. The U.S.-led forces later drove the Iraqi army out of Kuwait.

coalition bombing and the UN sanctions, Iraq's oil exports had dropped to less than 5 percent of what they had been before the war. These events made the oil fields in the Kurdish region even more valuable to Iraq. Hussein planned to quash the Kurdish rebellion and reclaim land that the Kurds had seized during the war.

After subduing Shiite revolts in southern Iraq, the Republican Guard quickly overwhelmed the Kurdistan Front. The international support that the front thought it would receive never ma-

terialized. U.S. president George Bush and British prime minister John Major, who before the Gulf War had urged the Iraqi opposition to overthrow Hussein, claimed that they didn't want to interfere with Iraq's internal situation. Weeks after the Gulf War ended, Iraqi forces had reclaimed control of Iraqi Kurdistan's main cities.

The Iraqi assault spurred a mass exodus from northern Kurdistan. Fearing another chemical weapons attack, Kurdish civilians, as well as most of the Kurdish pesh-

mergas, fled into the mountains for safety. Nearly one million Kurdish women and children headed for Iran and Turkey through snow, rain, and high winds. Those who went to Iran were allowed into the country, joining thousands of others who had fled there in the 1970s. But the Iranians didn't have enough money or resources to take care of the large refugee population.

When the Kurdish refugees arrived at the Turkish border, the government refused to let them into the country. Turkish president

Turgut Ozal didn't want to admit the displaced Kurds for fear of developing a large refugee problem similar to Iran's. He also worried that the refugees would stir rebellions among the Turkish Kurds or use Turkish camps as bases for launching future attacks against Saddam Hussein. Because the refugees weren't allowed into Turkey, they remained trapped in the hills and mountains in Iraq. Turkish military forces guarding the border attacked any refugees trying to enter the country.

OPERATION PROVIDE COMFORT

The Kurdish refugees were located in a region that was difficult to access, especially during the winter. Most roads were closed, due to mudslides and snow. As a result, it was nearly impossible for relief organizations to provide food, water, and shelter for the displaced Kurds. At one point, as many as 1,000 people—mainly children, elderly, and sick people—were dying each day. By the time the exodus was over, about 500,000

Kurdish refugees along the Iraqi-Turkish border beg for food from a Turkish truck (above). Kurds who fled to Iran (right) found that the Iranians were not equipped to handle a massive influx of refugees.

Kurds were near the Turkish border and more than 1 million had already crossed into Iran.

As the Kurdish refugee situation became worse and started to receive international attention, the United Nations and the U.S.-led coalition came under increasing criticism for failing to aid the refugees. In response to the problem and the criticism, the UN created Security Resolution 688 in April 1991. This was the first-ever UN resolution to address the Kurdish problem in detail. The resolution criticized the Iraqi government's repression and treatment of the Iraqi Kurds and demanded that the government allow **nongovernmental organizations (NGOs)** into the safe haven to offer aid to those in need.

In order to get the Kurds out of the mountains and away from the harsh conditions in those regions, the United States, Britain, and France established Operation Provide Comfort. The operation aimed to enable the United Nations High Commission for Refugees (UNHCR) and other NGOs to provide shelter, food, and medical supplies for the refugees along the Turkish border. To protect the Kurds from further attacks by Iraqi forces, Britain, France, and the United States also established a safe haven in northern Iraq. The safe haven covered approximately 65 percent of the Kurdish-populated region in northern Iraq. UN troops monitored the area and were responsible for protecting the nearly two million Iraqi Kurds located in the area. Under the stipulations of Operation Provide Comfort, Iraq could not interfere with the NGOs working in the safe haven. A no-fly zone, patrolled by U.S. and British jets, was established to prevent Hussein from sending planes into the area to bomb the Kurds. But Iraqi troops still controlled the Kurdish areas outside of the safe haven.

TURKS CHANGE TACTICS
While the plight of the Iraqi Kurds made international headlines, the Kurdish insurrection in Turkey and the Turkish government's treatment of its Kurdish population went largely unnoticed. But Kurdish nationalism was growing in Turkey. The Turkish military's violent repression of Kurdish civilians and the government's neglect of the depressed economic conditions in the Kurdish provinces had created more support for the PKK among the Kurdish population in southeastern Turkey. Many

© Ed Kashi

Kurds believed that the PKK was the only group interested in their plight.

The PKK's success and the flight of Kurdish refugees from Iraq brought Turkey's

Kurdish problem to the forefront. The Turkish government, fearing an uprising among its own Kurds, changed its tactics. While the Turkish military continued to battle the PKK, the government tried to discourage support for the separatist organization by appeasing the Kurdish population. In 1991 President Ozal and the National Assembly repealed the 1983 law that banned Kurds from speaking Kurdish. This was the first time since 1924 that Turkish Kurds were legally allowed to speak their own language. In accordance with this new freedom, the government released 43,000 Kurds who had been arrested for speaking Kurdish. Kurdish hopes were also rekindled when moderate Kurdish politicians from the People's Labour Party (HEP) gained seats in the National Assembly.

But Kurdish activists did not think the government had gone far enough. Turkey's partial repeal of the language law only enabled the Kurds to speak Kurdish in songs and in casual, everyday discussion—not in official business. Therefore, Turkish Kurds still did not have full freedom of speech.

Operation Provide Comfort

During and after the refugee crisis in northern Iraq, Operation Provide Comfort was a subject of heated debate. While some observers believed the operation was a groundbreaking humanitarian effort to protect refugees from a hostile government, critics suggested that the operation had military objectives rather than just humanitarian aims. These critics believed the Kurdish safe haven was used as a front for coalition forces to establish a presence in northern Iraq. They felt the coalition was using the Kurds as an excuse to remain in the region.

Other critics of Operation Provide Comfort pointed out the contradictions of the operation. They wondered why the coalition had not made similar efforts to protect Turkish Kurds from the hostile actions of the Turkish government. They also noted that refugee operations in Iran received only half the funding of those on the Iraq-Turkey border. These contradictions led many to suggest that the United States, which led the coalition, was motivated more by political concerns than humanitarian ones.

For the Turks, Operation Provide Comfort and the Kurdish safe haven created a dilemma. The Turkish government was critical of the effort, claiming that it enabled Kurdish separatists to reorganize under the protection of the United States and its allies. But Turkish officials also wanted the operation to remain in place and keep the Iraqi Kurds out of Turkey. Ultimately, the Turkish government decided it would rather have the Kurds united in northern Iraq than spilling over the borders into Turkey. This was also the case with the governments in other countries with Kurdish populations. Iranian and Syrian officials didn't want more Kurds to migrate to their countries and supported the idea of having a safe haven in Iraq. These officials also didn't want those in the safe haven to become powerful enough to break away from Iraq, since this could spark uprisings in their own countries.

Under Turkish laws, the Kurds were still banned from speaking or using Kurdish on TV and radio broadcasts and in newspapers, magazines, and books. In fact, use of the words "Kurd" or "Kurdistan" was still illegal.

Turkish Kurds had reason to be skeptical, because the government's policy toward the Kurds had two faces. After Ozal lifted the censorship and language laws in 1991, the Turkish military deployed about 200,000 troops in southeastern Turkey to displace Kurdish civilians from their villages. The goal was to break down the growth of Kurdish nationalism by eliminating the PKK and asserting military control over the region. The Turkish government said it was leading a legitimate fight to suppress the PKK, which it believed was undermining its authority and threatening the stability of Turkey. According to the government, the PKK was not only a threat to individual Turkish citizens and political leaders but was also a danger to the country's overall sense of national cohesion.

Stepping up its efforts to crush the insurrection, the Turkish military burned forests in eastern Turkey to locate PKK members. As the Turkish forces swept through the mountains in search of the PKK, many PKK fighters fled to Iran and Iraq. To keep Turkish Kurds from organizing pro-Kurdish groups and supporting the PKK, the regional governor moved, spread out, or divided up Kurdish villages, forcing thousands of Kurds to flee their homes. The Turkish government claimed it displaced more than 200,000 people to rid southeastern Turkey of terrorist groups that were forming or in

Although President Turgut Ozal (above left) *made some efforts to appease Turkish Kurds, he also stepped up efforts to destroy the PKK and to root out Kurdish separatism* (above).

operation there. The Kurds claimed the number of people displaced was even greater. In response to the Turkish offensive, PKK fighters ambushed Turkish troops and killed village guards throughout the region.

The Turkish government resorted to other repressive tactics to stifle the Kurds. In March 1992, at a nonviolent Kurdish demonstration during Newroz, Turkish security forces opened fire on the demonstrators, killing more than 70 people. In April the Turkish government established the Anti-Terror Law, which forbids "written and oral propaganda . . . aiming at damaging the indivisible unity of the State of the Turkish Republic." The law enabled the state to ban Kurdish newspapers and books as propaganda and to arrest proponents of Kurdish rights. In addition, freedom of speech was restricted among Kurdish students, denying Kurdish children the right to speak or learn Kurdish. Kurdish children were also forced to pledge their allegiance to Turkey. Meanwhile, there was an increase in the harassment and torture of the human rights

Kurdish children are often forced to take part in Turkish celebrations.

monitors and journalists.

At the same time, the Turkish military also began to launch attacks in northern Iraq. After the Gulf War, many PKK members had established bases in northern Iraq, where they hoped to continue operations while soliciting support from the Iraqi Kurds who lived in and around the safe haven area. The Turkish government believed that the attacks would prevent the PKK from regrouping and gaining support from Iraqi Kurds. The gov-

ernment also enlisted the KDP and the PUK to help fight the PKK. In return the Turkish government provided the Iraqi Kurds with much-needed medical supplies and food. As a result, Iraqi Kurds ended up aiding the Turkish military in its fight against Turkish Kurds.

KURDISH ELECTIONS IN IRAQ
Meanwhile, in northern Iraq, the Iraqi Kurds and Saddam Hussein were locked in a stalemate. Neither the Kurds nor Hussein were happy

with the situation in northern Iraq. The Kurds did not have the means to fight Hussein's troops, and Hussein could not completely subdue the Kurds without being punished by coalition forces. So in mid-1991, Massoud Barzani began secret negotiations with Hussein on an autonomy agreement that would give the Kurds freedom of speech, a limited amount of self-rule, their own legislative council, and an executive council. There was still a dispute over who would control Kirkuk, however. Barzani wanted Kirkuk to be part of autonomous Kurdistan. Hussein, on the other hand, wanted to retain control of the oil-rich province. Barzani also demanded democracy in Iraq.

Hussein demanded something in return for giving the Kurds an autonomous region. He wanted the Kurdistan Front disbanded and its

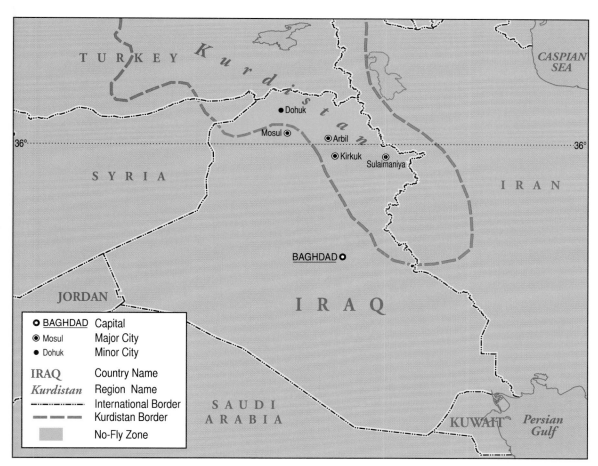

The no-fly zone runs between the thirty-sixth parallel and the Iraqi-Turkish border.

radio and TV stations closed. He also wanted the Kurds to stop negotiations and contacts with other countries and to support his government against its enemies. In addition, Hussein demanded that the Kurdistan Front give up all its heavy weapons. The front was split on these negotiations. While Barzani believed it necessary to reach an agreement with Hussein to end the conflict, Jalal Talabani opposed the demands made by the Iraqi leader.

As negotiations continued, the Iraqi government placed an economic embargo on northern Iraq, halting the flow of food and supplies to that region. Hussein also removed all government employees and administrative staff from northern Iraq. The Kurdish region outside of the safe haven was hit hardest by the embargo, and many Kurds fled to the safe haven for relief. Hussein then moved more troops into northern Iraq, along the borders of the safe haven.

Eventually, the KDP and the PUK rejected all of Hussein's demands and resumed their fight against the Iraqi regime. Hussein planned a major offensive but backed down after a warning from the United States. In April 1992, with the autonomy deal dead, the Kurdistan Front established a **de facto government** in the safe haven, which was still protected by U.S. and British jets. Barzani hoped that this government could provide leadership and services for citizens in the region. He also hoped that the no-fly zone restrictions would protect the region from Hussein's forces.

In May 1992, the Kurds in the safe haven held their first democratic elections in Arbil. The local population elected a parliament, which was made up mainly of PUK and KDP members. In the elections for a leader of the

© Ed Kashi

After years of rivalry, KDP leader Massoud Barzani (second from right) and PUK leader Jalal Talabani (center, next to boy) agreed to share governing duties in the Kurdish autonomous region.

region, Barzani beat Jalal Talabani by 466,819 votes to 441,057. But Barzani didn't have the majority of votes in each region. Before another vote could be held, the two groups reached an agreement to divide the governing of the region between them. The chairman of the executive council would be from the KDP and the deputy would be from the PUK, while the chairman of the national council would be from the PUK and the deputy would be from the KDP.

BROKEN PROMISES

Despite ongoing clashes between the army and the PKK in southeastern Turkey, the Turkish government appeared to adopt a new position toward the Kurds in late 1992 and 1993. Turgut Ozal publicly acknowledged the Kurdish question and indicated that he would deal with the issue of the PKK and Kurdish separatism. This was the first time a Turkish leader had openly discussed the Kurdish situation in Turkey. In a six-page letter to Turkish prime minister Suleyman Demirel in early 1993, Ozal discussed his proposal for holding open de-

Tansu Ciller's View

In 1994 then-Turkish prime minister Tansu Ciller outlined the Turkish government's view of the Kurdish situation and the relationship between the Kurds and the PKK. "Officially, in Turkey there are three minorities, Greek Christians, Armenian Christians, and Jews. This official minority status is a legal legacy of the 1923 treaty of Lausanne, which viewed Muslims in the newly formed Turkish republic as a whole, and defined minority status strictly to protect the religious rights of these three groups. But as a unitary nation state built from more than 20 ethnic backgrounds, who have completely intermingled, no special privileges have ever been attached to any group because of ethnic background, race, or geographic location. We are all first-class citizens. Among these groups are Kurds . . . full citizens of the republic, active in every walk of life, living in every region, and fully integrated publicly, privately, and politically. The PKK terrorist campaign for separatism cannot relate to their needs or aspirations. indeed, they continue to be the greatest victims of PKK brutality. Our goal is greater liberty for each and every individual."

bate with the Kurds. The government's new stance encouraged PKK leader Abdullah Ocalan to declare a **unilateral cease-fire** in March to find out if the Turkish government would stop fighting and start negotiating.

After the announcement of the cease-fire, Ocalan, apparently ready to give up the armed struggle, dropped his demands for Kurdish independence and said he would accept recognition of Kurdish

rights and cultural freedom. The government refused to accept the cease-fire, but it did announce a program to revive the economy of the Kurdish region. President Ozal believed that economic improvements would help counter the influence of the PKK and stifle Kurdish nationalism. But Ozal—who appeared willing to negotiate with the Kurds—died of a heart attack in April 1993. Some people speculate that he was killed by his own government or the Turkish military—the people who were opposed to his plans to negotiate and work with the Kurds.

After Ozal died, the negotiations fell apart. Neither the new president, Suleyman Demirel, nor the military had any intentions of negotiating with the PKK. Calling the group a terrorist organization, Demirel ignored the cease-fire and ended negotiations with the PKK. After PKK fighters ambushed and killed a group of unarmed Turkish soldiers, the army-dominated National Security Council strengthened martial law in the Kurdish provinces. The PKK responded with a renewed wave of terrorism, launching attacks on tourist sites and kidnapping foreign nationals.

Under Demirel and his prime minister, Tansu Ciller, Turkey seemed more committed than ever to suppressing the Kurds. In 1994 the Turkish military launched a new offensive in southeastern Turkey, sending troops to kill PKK guerillas and clear Kurdish villages. The military also forcibly deported more than 150,000 Kurdish civilians from their villages. The renewed crackdown by the Turkish military also included attacks in northern Iraq to destroy PKK bases located in the area. Although the army claimed that PKK guerrillas were their target, many Kurdish civilians in northern Iraq were killed during these raids. The moves by the Turkish military brought strong criticism from Europe and the United States.

During the same period, the government also took constitutional action against the Kurds. In June 1994, Turkey's constitutional court banned the Democracy Party (DEP), a pro-Kurdish party whose members had criticized Turkish policy toward the Kurds. The government claimed that the DEP was a political wing of the PKK. Six members of the party serving in the Turkish National Assembly were arrested and charged with advocating separatism.

RENEWED RIVALRY

Shortly after the establishment of the Kurdish government in Iraqi Kurdistan, the relationship between the KDP and PUK began to dissolve. In December 1994, continuing hostilities between Barzani and Talabani developed into war. The conflict was caused by the fact that the KDP was collecting major revenues from border traffic between northern Iraq and Turkey. Talabani and the PUK wanted their share of the money. The fighting led

You must be clear. . . . Either you are yellow, which is KDP, or you are green, which is PUK. Go to the wrong area, and you will be persecuted.
—An Iraqi Kurd

to the collapse of the parliamentary system of the autonomous region. The two parties signed a cease-fire in early 1995, but fighting resumed in 1996, when Talabani and his forces, with support from Iran, took control of Arbil—the unofficial capital of the autonomous region—and kicked out the KDP.

The renewed fighting set

KDP fighters take position on a hill in northern Iraq. With support from Iraqi forces, the KDP was able to defeat PUK fighters and regain control of Arbil. But the fighting between the two parties only brought more suffering for Kurdish civilians in the region.

off a new round of alliances that once again brought Iraq and Iran back into the picture. In August 1996, the KDP called on Saddam Hussein for help against the KDP. Iraqi forces backed the KDP in its efforts to push the PUK out of Arbil and Sulaimaniyeh. During the fighting, Hussein sent about 30,000 Iraqi troops to assist in the assault. This incursion clearly violated the UN-established no-fly zones. The PUK, which was heavily armed and supported by Iran, didn't put up a big fight. Talabani was furious that Barzani had joined forces with Hussein, but Barzani claimed that he was protecting the KDP against Iranian attacks.

After Hussein's soldiers took over Arbil and Suleimaniyeh, the United States launched an attack to punish Hussein for violating the no-fly zones. U.S. planes dropped bombs on Iraqi air defense targets south of Baghdad, and U.S. ships based in the Persian Gulf launched at least 20 cruise missiles. Iraqi forces imme- diately withdrew, but Kurdish sources claimed that some members of the Iraqi secret service stayed behind to root out any of Hussein's opponents.

The KDP-Iraqi offensive led to the collapse of the safe haven. Thousands of PUK fighters Kurds fled to the Iranian border in early September 1996, along with members of Iraqi opposition groups based in the north. The fighting also caused an exodus of humanitarian aid agencies from northern Iraq. Within two weeks of the

KDP-Iraqi takeover of Arbil and Sulaimaniyeh, at least 25 of the 51 relief organizations had shut down, including those overseeing the command center for Operation Provide Comfort. The departure of NGO workers left hundreds of thousands of Kurds, who had been dependent upon U.S. and allied aid, without necessary food and medicine.

KURDISH LEADER ARRESTED

Throughout 1997 and 1998, the Turkish government's battle with the PKK continued. Even though the PKK had renounced separatism, the Turks still did everything they could to subdue the group. In March 1997, about 40,000 Turkish troops led a large-scale attack to hunt down PKK guerillas in southeastern Turkey. By May 15,000 to 30,000 Turkish troops were in northern Iraq, running a massive operation to eliminate PKK bases in the region. That month, the KDP joined forces with Turkish troops in another military operation against the PKK. Turkey claimed its involvement was part of a humanitarian mission to protect Kurds in northern Iraq from

> *"There is no Kurdish question in Turkey. What we face today is a bloody terrorist campaign aimed at the stability and territorial integrity of Turkey."*
> —Suleyman Demirel

the PKK. UN secretary general Kofi Anan asked Turkish officials to remove troops from Iraqi Kurdistan, but they refused.

The Turkish military launched another major offensive in late September, sending more troops to northern Iraq to wipe out PKK bases. Turkish president Suleyman Demirel is reported to have told an Anatolian news agency that "Turkey has the right to defend its territory . . . . There is no Iraqi control in northern Iraq, there are terrorists there."

The operation lasted until October, when Turkey pulled thousands of troops out of northern Iraq and began fighting PKK rebels in mountainous areas of Turkey's southeastern provinces. But about 8,000 Turkish troops remained in northern Iraq to police the area and to subdue PKK rebels.

In November 1997, Turkish troops were sent to another area in northern Iraq, near the border with Iran, to quash an attack by the PUK against the KDP. Turkey claimed that the PUK was collaborating with the PKK and that the PUK attacks had broken an October cease-fire between the PUK and the KDP. In December 20,000 Turkish troops joined forces with about 8,000 KDP forces to launch a new offensive against PKK rebels in northern Iraq. In December 1997, Demirel told reporters, "We are determined to defend our territorial integrity until the end."

In late 1998 and early 1999, the Turks dealt the Kurdish insurgency a major blow. In November 1998, Italian officials arrested Abdullah Ocalan in Rome, Italy, when he tried to seek political asylum in the country. Turkish officials wanted Ocalan extradited to Turkey to face charges of **treason**, but Italian officials refused because the PKK leader could be executed if found guilty. (Italy does not use the death penalty and will not extradite people to a country that does.)

The Italians eventually released Ocalan, and he again went into hiding. But in February 1999, Turkish commandos captured Ocalan in Kenya and returned him to Turkey, where he was placed on the prison island of Imrali. PKK supporters throughout Europe protested the arrest.

In May 1999, Ocalan was put on trial by the Turkish government and charged with treason. Ocalan's lawyers claimed that there was no way he could receive a fair trial in Turkey. Turkish prosecutors were pushing for the death penalty for Ocalan, despite the Kurdish leader's offer to negotiate an end to the fighting in return for sparing his life. PKK guerrillas warned that if their leader was put to death, the violence would only intensify. Before his sentencing, the Kurdish leader said, "I do not accept the charge of treason . . . . I believe I've struggled for the unity of the land and a free life." On June 29 the Turkish court found Ocalan guilty and sentenced him to death. ⊕

A bound Abdullah Ocalan sits between two masked Turkish commandos. After capturing Ocalan in Kenya, Turkish authorities brought him back to Turkey to face trial.

Reuters/HO/Archive Photos

CHAPTER 5

WHAT'S BEING DONE TO SOLVE THE PROBLEM

Although government leaders in Turkey, Iran, and Iraq periodically discuss the Kurdish problem, they are doing very little to find a peaceful solution. Their energy is directed more toward fighting Kurdish factions and suppressing Kurdish nationalism than establishing a dialogue with these groups. As a result, plans to solve the Kurdish situation are generally nonexistent within these countries.

Ultimately, the governments of Turkey, Iraq, and Iran prefer to deny the existence of the Kurds and try to assimilate them into their respective societies. Although each government has relaxed laws that restrict Kurdish rights, the Kurds are still denied most cultural, social, political, and, in many

cases, economic rights. The fear that giving in to Kurdish demands will lead to a wider ethnic upheaval prevents these governments from even contemplating negotiation. The only time they will negotiate with the Kurds is when it will help them undermine each other.

Turkish officials first formally acknowledged the "Kurdish problem" in the early 1990s, a major step for a nation that had long denied that Kurdish people even existed. The loosening of language laws, though more of a symbolic gesture than a true reform, was another step forward. Some Turkish politicians have even suggested making economic reforms and granting the Kurds cultural rights in southeastern Turkey. While such sugges-

tions show more concern for ending the Kurdish insurrection than for dealing with the aspirations of the Kurdish people, they still represent a step forward.

Yet nationalist Turks usually criticize any suggestions that the government give the Kurds more rights. Furthermore, the government and the military still consider the PKK a terrorist group and show no interest in negotiating with more moderate Kurdish parties, such as the People's Democracy Party (HADEP). The Turkish government claims that it will not negotiate with the Kurds until the PKK has been defeated. Meanwhile, Turkish security forces continue to harass and abuse Kurdish activists and journalists. For the Turks, the belief that giving

Although no longer living in Kurdistan, Kurds throughout the world remain involved in the Kurdish conflict. In Lebanon (right), *protesters show their support for Abdullah Ocalan. In Germany* (below), *Kurdish immigrants march in support of the PKK.*

in to one minority will lead to the disintegration of the country remains as strong as ever.

In Iraq Saddam Hussein has negotiated with the Kurds and granted them some rights but only under pressure from the international community. Hussein is not motivated by the needs of the Kurds but rather by what he can gain from supporting one Kurdish faction against another. In addition, Hussein still sends troops to attack Kurds in the north and has said several times that he'll no longer abide by the

CHAPTER 5 *What's Being Done to Solve the Problem*

> *Perhaps the biggest obstacle to resolving the Kurdish conflict is the infighting between Kurdish factions, which has accounted for thousands of deaths and is responsible for keeping the Kurds divided.*

no-fly zones. The Baathist government also continues to Arabize northern Iraq by forcibly removing Kurdish residents from cities such as Mosul and Kirkuk. Some Kurdish politicians have been assassinated. Despite making some concessions to the Kurds, the Iraqi regime clearly views them as a threatening presence that needs to be assimilated or eliminated.

One country where positive dialogue has taken place is Iran, where President Mohammad Khatami, elected in 1997, has shown signs of addressing the Kurdish problem. During his first year in office, Khatami allowed more minority publications to begin printing and gave writers greater freedom of expression, stating that journalists should be able to write freely without being punished for their views. The Iranian president also agreed to meet with Iranian Kurds to discuss the Kurdish situa-

tion and said he will make reforms to give Iranian Kurds more cultural and religious freedom. Recently, a Kurdish governor was appointed to administer Iranian Kurdistan. Despite these positive signs, critics don't believe Iranian Kurds will ever enjoy autonomy. As proof that the Iranian government has a long way to go, these critics point out that Kurdish politicians opposed to the Iranian government are still being imprisoned and even executed.

Perhaps the biggest obstacle to resolving the Kurdish conflict is the infighting between Kurdish factions, which has accounted for thousands of deaths and is responsible for keeping the Kurds divided. In the fall of 1998, after nearly four years of fighting, the Iraqi Kurds took a major step toward removing this obstacle. In September Massoud Barzani and Jalal Talabani met in Washington, D.C., where they signed an agreement to form

a transitional power-sharing authority that would take over until a regional assembly is elected for Iraqi Kurdistan.

HUMANITARIAN AID

While the Kurdish dilemma remains unsolved, humanitarian aid organizations are working for peace and security for the Kurds in the region. The majority of NGOs and aid organizations are based in Turkey and Iraq, where they provide food, water, shelter, medicines, and health care to civilians. But the number of organizations in these regions has fluctuated over the past few years, due to outbreaks of fighting between Kurdish groups and attacks led by regional governments and coalition nations.

By early 1999, there were still at least several dozen NGOs and relief agencies working in Turkey and Iraq. U.S.-based relief, development, and refugee agencies operating in Turkey and Iraq included CARE, Catholic Relief Services, Direct Relief International, and Doctors Without Borders, as well as International Catholic Migration Service and International Medical Services for

Health. Other groups working in Turkey include World Learning, Pathfinder International, and the American Jewish Joint Distribution Committee. The UNHCR, Human Rights Watch, and World Food Program are also working in these regions. They oversee the security of refugees, monitor human rights issues, and collect and distribute food and water to refugees and displaced persons, especially along the Iraq-Turkey border and the Iraq-Iran border.

The focus in the Kurdish area of Iraq has been rehabilitating the communities that have been damaged by the fighting. One group that has helped Kurds in northern Iraq rehabilitate their communities is the Kurdistan Children's Fund (KCF). A British organization, KCF has built houses for more than 2,000 people, supplied food and clothes to orphanages and poor families, provided work-skills training for the unemployed, and established educational programs for children. Habitat, part of the UN's program in Iraq, is also active in the Kurdish enclave.

Meanwhile, human rights advocacy groups such as Amnesty International and Human Rights Watch are working to inform people about the Kurdish situation. Both groups issue reports

Kurdish children in northern Iraq work to rebuild their village. Over the past few years, a number of NGOs have worked to help improve lives of Kurdish civilians in northern Iraq.

The Kurds and the International Community

Since the beginning of the twentieth century, European nations and the United States have simultaneously aided the Kurds and the governments that suppress them. Like the governments in Turkey, Iran, and Iraq, the United States and other nations have used the Kurds to pursue their own political interests in the Middle East. All too often, the Kurds have taken a back seat to these countries' greater strategic interests. As a result, the international community's Middle Eastern policies have been among the obstacles preventing the Kurds from gaining greater rights.

The trend continues. Take, for example, the current policy of the United States toward the Kurds. The United States helped establish a safe haven for the Kurds in northern Iraq after the Gulf War, and U.S. jets continue to patrol the no-fly zone in that region. Since the end of the Gulf War, the United States has also encouraged Kurdish efforts to destabilize the Iraqi regime. In December 1998, U. S. president Bill Clinton stated that his administration would provide financial and military support to antigovernment groups in Iraq—including the Kurds—that worked to overthrow Saddam Hussein.

At the same time, however, the United States has contributed millions of dollars of foreign aid each year to Turkey. A 1995 report by the U.S. State Department stated that U.S. weapons have been used by the Turks against the PKK. "It is highly likely that such equipment was used in support of the evacuation and/or destruction of villages," the report claimed. William Schulz, executive director of Amnesty International, USA, said in a *60 Minutes* broadcast that in 1996 the U.S. was providing Turkey with $320 million in aid, most of which would be used by the Turkish government to persecute the Kurds. Therefore, as the United States was providing aid for Iraqi Kurds in northern Iraq, it was also funding and supplying Turkey's military campaign against Turkish Kurds. The United States has also refrained from criticizing Turkey's human rights abuses and press censorship.

detailing human rights abuses against Kurds in Iraq, Iran, and Turkey. In these reports, the organizations urge the governments of these countries to put a stop to the violent suppression of the Kurds. These groups also campaign to get international governments and organizations to condemn human rights abuses against the Kurdish population. Amnesty International, for example, has urged the United States to ensure that U.S. weapons sold to Turkey are not used against Kurdish civilians. Human Rights Watch has asked the international community to protest Turkish press censorship and to condemn violence against journalists who criticize the government's Kurdish policies.

GROUPS AND ORGANIZATIONS

Since regional governments continue to restrict cultural expression among the Kurds,

Political and military leaders in the United States believe that these contradictory policies help to achieve two goals. Supporting the Iraqi Kurds helps to destabilize the government of Saddam Hussein, whom the United States views as a threat to the Middle East. On the other hand, supporting Turkey and funding its war against the PKK strengthens a country that the United States views as a stabilizing influence in the Middle East. The U.S. military also wants to be able to use Turkish air force bases for patrolling the Iraqi no-fly zones. For the Kurds, these policies send mixed messages. While the KDP and the PUK are recognized as legitimate political groups fighting a repressive government, the PKK is labeled as a terrorist group threatening a democratic government.

European policy toward the Kurds is less contradictory but still inconsistent. Certain European nations have recently been vocal in their concerns about Turkey's human rights abuses, in particular its treatment of the Kurds. The prime minister of Italy even called for dialogue between Turkey and its Kurds. This criticism is significant, because Turkey wants to become part of the European Union, an organization of European states that handles economic and political issues on the continent. Still, other European nations—such as Britain, France, and Germany—have followed the example of the United States and have muted their criticism of Turkey. And most European leaders have condemned the activities of the PKK.

U.S. and European leaders are in agreement on one aspect of the Kurdish situation. None of these leaders wants to see the creation of an independent Kurdistan encompassing land in Turkey, Iran, Syria, and Iraq. The international community wants to maintain the territorial integrity of these nations, and most leaders believe that the creation of such a state would only lead to more turmoil in the region. As a result, U.S. support of the Iraqi Kurds will only go so far. Many Kurds find the lack of international support for Kurdish independence difficult to accept. They don't understand why Kurds can't have their own state, especially when so many other ethnic nationalities have gained independence over the last few years.

there are a number of groups around the world that are working to preserve, protect, and celebrate Kurdish culture. The Kurdish Library and Museum, based in Brooklyn, New York, is a research center that holds regular exhibits on Kurdish history, culture, and contemporary affairs. The Kurdish Library also produces two publications, *The International Journal of Kurdish Studies* and *Kurdish Life*. One of the goals of the Kurdish Library is to dispel the myths and propaganda about the Kurds that circulate in the U.S. and foreign media.

Because of the large Kurdish population in Europe, there are dozens of Kurdish publications printed in Sweden, Germany, the Netherlands, and France. These publications aim to foster awareness on Kurdish issues, promote Kurdish culture, and deal with human rights issues. *Dengê* is a Kurdish women's magazine that is published in Sweden, while *Melbend* is a monthly newsletter printed by the Kurdish Cultural Center in London. *Kurdistan News* is a bimonthly publication of the International Association for Human Rights in Kurdistan, printed in Germany. The Kurdish Study Group at Deakin University in Australia publishes the *Kurdish Newsletter*.

In addition, more than 40 publications dealing with Kurdish issues, culture, history, and folklore are printed legally and illegally in the Middle East. These publications appear in many different languages, including Turkish, Greek, Arabic, and the northern and southern dialects of Kurdish—Kurmanji and Sorani.

There are also a number of institutions that offer Kurdish language studies programs worldwide, including the Kurdish Institute in Brussels, the Kurdish Cultural Center in London, the Kurdish Institute in Paris, and the Washington Kurdish Institute in Washington, D.C. In recent years, these facilities have hosted conferences, seminars, and discussions on Kurdish issues and culture.

CONFLICT RESOLUTION

In July 1998, the Washington Kurdish Institute held a Kurdish Conflict Resolution Forum, which brought together human rights officials, NGO workers, U.S. government officials, representatives of Kurdish political parties, conflict resolution and Middle East experts, residents from Kurdish and Middle Eastern communities, and the general public. During the two-day forum, this group discussed the current situations in Iran, Iraq, and Turkey and came up with a number of recommendations to resolve the conflicts in these countries.

Because of Turkey's democratic form of government and its well-educated population, forum attendees felt that Turkey had the greatest possibility of changing. To resolve the Kurdish problem in Turkey, the forum suggested that the PKK abandon the use of violence as a political tool and acknowledge Turkey's security concerns and the inviolability of its borders. At the same time, forum participants recommended that the Turkish government lift martial law in southeastern Turkey, revoke the powers of the regional governor to restrict expression and association, remove restrictions on Kurdish cultural expression, allow Kurdish-language television and radio broadcasts, and disband the village guard system. In addition, forum participants concluded that the United States needs to restrict sales of weapons to Turkey until the country cleans up its human rights record.

The role of the Turkish people was also addressed. According to forum participant Mehdi Zana, the former mayor of Diyarbakir, "the solution is in the hands of the Turkish people. They have to accept the rights of the Kurds. They need to force their government to come to terms with the reality of the Kurds . . . if they continue to call the problem simply 'terrorism,' there will not be a solution to the challenge that we face."

Recommendations for Iraq concentrated on two issues. Forum participants first discussed the conflict between the PUK and the KDP. To resolve this conflict, the forum

> *"The solution is in the hands of the Turkish people. They have to accept the rights of the Kurds."*
> —Mehdi Zana, former mayor of Diyarbakir

suggested that the international community promote the establishment of a political framework to bring PUK and KDP members together. At the same time, PUK and KDP members were urged to identify ways of distributing trade revenues among the two groups and to establish joint ministries and service departments. The second issue covered was the conflict between the Kurds and the government. Many felt that the best way to improve the Kurdish situation in Iraq was to establish a democratic form of government. It was suggested that the United States make the Iraqi Kurds the foundation for opposition to Saddam Hussein. Finally, forum participants recommended that the international community make greater efforts to protect the Iraqi Kurds and enable humanitarian relief to reach northern Iraq.

Although forum participants were cautious about the reforms of President Khatami in Iran, they did express hope that the reforms would enable Iranian Kurds to become more involved in the country's political life. Many of the forum's recommendations for Iran related to the establishment of conditions within Iran that would facilitate dialogue between Kurds and Iranians. The forum recommended the creation of a Kurdish-Iranian center to promote "peace through culture." The center would work to foster reconciliation, dialogue, and cultural exchanges between Iranian Kurds and the people of Iran. Other suggestions included supporting the movement for democracy and civil society in Iran, including the development of a free press.

At the end of the conference, panelists discussed the creation of a Kurdish conflict resolution task force, which an international committee of conflict resolution experts would advise. This task force would consist of Kurds living in the region and abroad.

Ultimately, the participants in the forum recognized that Kurdish independence is a long way off. Instead, Kurds must focus on the most pressing issues facing them—easing government repression, solving conflicts between Kurdish political groups, and gaining greater cultural rights. To achieve these goals, the Kurds and the governments of the region must be willing to renounce violence and establish a meaningful dialogue that respects the needs of all involved. Unless this happens, the fighting and bloodshed will continue. ⊕

EPILOGUE*

By the fall of 1999, the Kurdish issue remained in the spotlight in Turkey. Daily clashes between the PKK and the Turkish military continued after a Turkish court sentenced Abdullah Ocalan to death in June. But on August 3, 1999, the condemned PKK leader called for his supporters to end their fight against the Turkish government and to leave Turkey by September 1. In an official statement responding to the request, PKK leaders stated that the group had agreed to stop the fighting and instead pursue a political campaign against the Turkish government. The statement expressed hope that the decision to stop the fighting would pressure the Turkish government into making concessions to the country's Kurdish minority. The Turkish government responded to the announcement by rejecting any future negotiations with the PKK. Turkish authorities also said that the military would continue its campaign to rid the southeast of PKK guerrillas. Despite increasing pressure from U.S. and European leaders to peacefully resolve the Kurdish issue, Turkey continued to maintain its stance.

In northern Iraq, meanwhile, the KDP and the PUK have been making efforts to abide by the cease-fire signed in September 1998. Although the Kurdish autonomous region continues to be split into areas of KDP control and areas of PUK control, there has been little fighting between the groups. As a result, the Kurdish regional government has been able to concentrate on rebuilding the region's infrastructure. But conflict in the region remains. KDP leaders claim that the PKK has attacked Iraqi Kurds. The leaders believe that the PUK has assisted the PKK by allowing PKK fighters to set up bases in their territory. U.S. and British jets continue to protect the no-fly zone over northern Iraq. In the fall of 1999, new Kurd-related tension arose between Turkey and Iran. The Turkish government claimed that the Iranian government had been allowing PKK fighters to seek refuge along the Turkish-Iranian border. The Iranian government denied that it harbors PKK fighters.

* Please note: The information presented in *Kurdistan: Region under Siege* was current at the time of the book's publication. For the most up-to-date information on the conflict, check for articles in the international section of U.S. daily newspapers. The *Economist*, a weekly magazine, is also a good source for up-to-date information. You may also wish to access, via the Internet, other sources of information about Kurdistan: Political Resources on the Net-Kurdistan, at <http://www.agora.stm.it/politic/kurdistan.htm>, directs you to a variety of websites devoted to Kurdish issues.

CHRONOLOGY

ca. 4300 B.C. The Hurrian culture settles in the mountains of what would become Kurdistan.

2000 B.C. Indo-European tribes migrate to Kurdistan.

300 B.C. Kurdish kingdoms established in the mountainous regions of Kurdistan.

A.D. 600s The Arabs take control of much of the Middle East, including Kurdistan. Kurds accept the Islamic religion and Kurdish soldiers fight in Arab armies.

1100s Sultan Saladin founds the Ayyubid dynasty. During the Third Crusade, his armies reestablish Muslim control over Jerusalem.

1400s The Ottomans become the most powerful force in the region, establishing control over much of Anatolia, Kurdistan, and Mesopotamia.

1505–1508 Shah Ismail, head of the Safavid dynasty, captures Kurdish and Ottoman territory in Mesopotamia.

1514 Ottoman armies defeat Safavid troops at the battle of Chaldiran. The Kurdo-Ottoman pact splits Kurdistan into 16 territories, over which Kurdish leaders have control.

1806 The first major Kurdish revolt against the Ottomans occurs in the principality of Baban. The revolt is put down by Ottoman forces, but other uprisings follow.

1880 Sheikh Ubaidullah leads a Kurdish uprising in Persia. Ottoman and Persian forces combine to squash the revolt.

1898 *Kurdistan*, the first Kurdish journal, is established.

1908 The Young Turks overthrow the government of the sultan, and the CUP takes over the leadership of the Ottoman Empire. Kurdish nationalism grows as intellectuals begin forming Kurdish clubs.

1909 The CUP bans all non-Turkish members from the organization. Kurdish organizations and publications become illegal.

1915–1918 The Ottomans enter World War I. The Kurds help Turkish forces defeat the Russians and Armenians. Defeated on all other fronts, the Ottoman sultan is forced to sign a peace treaty with the Allies, who want to carve up the empire.

1918 In his Fourteen Points Declaration, U.S. president Woodrow Wilson declares that nationalities under Turkish rule, including the Kurds, should be able to pursue autonomy.

1919 Led by Sheikh Mahmoud Berezenji, Kurdish tribes in Mesopotamia revolt.

1920–1922 The Ottoman leadership signs the Treaty of Sèvres, which promises the Kurds an autonomous Kurdistan. But the Ottoman government falls, and the provisional government under Mustafa Kemal rejects the treaty. British-held territory in Mesopotamia becomes the Kingdom of Iraq. Under the leadership of Agha Simko, Kurdish tribes in Persia threaten the Persian leadership's control of the country.

1923 Sheikh Mahmoud leads another uprising in Iraq but is defeated and exiled by British troops. General Reza Khan comes to power in Persia and begins to suppress Kurdish tribes.

1923–1927 Turkey signs the Treaty of Lausanne, which declares Turkey a republic and gives the Turks control over Kurdish land. The Turkish government under Ataturk begins a massive campaign to suppresses Kurdish nationalism, leading to Kurdish revolts. The League of Nations decides that the province of Mosul should remain part of Iraq.

1932 Iraq gains independence from Britain. Iraqi Kurds rise in revolt, but the uprisings are put down by the Iraqi government. In Turkey the government enacts a law that calls for the displacement and assimilation of the Kurdish population.

1937 Turkey, Iran, and Iraq sign the Saadabad Treaty, which aims to suppress Kurdish separatism.

1945 Iraqi and Iranian Kurds form the KDPI.

1946–1947 The KDPI establishes the Mahabad Republic. Within a year, the Iranian government crushes the republic and executes many KDPI leaders.

1958 Iraqi general Abdul Karim Qasim and the Free Officers overthrow the Iraqi monarchy. Qasim invites Mustafa Barzani to return to Iraq and makes reforms that benefit the Kurds.

1961–1963 To gain autonomy, Iraqi Kurds launch a rebellion against the Iraqi government. The Baath Party overthrows President Qasim but continues the war against the Kurds. The new Iraqi president begins the Arabization program.

1966–1969 The Turkish government cracks down on Kurdish journals and other expressions of Kurdish identity. Violent treatment by Turkish commandos spurs Kurdish protests. In Iraq the government declares a cease-fire with the Kurds and begins negotiations. After another military coup, the new Iraqi government breaks off talks with the Kurds and resumes the war. Iranian Kurds launch a revolt against the government of the shah.

1971 The Iraqi government and the KDP sign the March 11 Agreement, which promises autonomy for Iraqi Kurds.

1974–1975 Iraq establishes the Autonomous Region of Kurdistan, but Barzani rejects the autonomy deal and war resumes between the KDP and the government. After Iran and Iraq sign the Algiers Agreement, Iran stops supporting the KDP. Iraq defeats the KDP and causes a massive exodus.

1978 In response to increasing unrest in southeastern Turkey, the Turkish government declares martial law in 13 southeastern provinces. Abdullah Ocalan establishes the PKK.

1979 The shah of Iran is forced to leave the country, and the Iranian government is taken over by Islamic fundamentalists.

1980 The Iran-Iraq War begins. In Turkey the Turkish military overthrows the government and increases its suppression of Kurdish nationalism.

1984 The PKK begins its guerrilla war against the Turkish government.

1987 The KDP, PUK, and other Kurdish groups in Iraq unite to form the Kurdistan Front. Iranian troops and Kurdistan Front forces advance into Iraq. Iraq launches chemical attacks against Kurds.

1988 The Iran-Iraq war ends. In Turkey the government gives the governor-general of the Kurdish provinces the power to evacuate villages and deport the population.

1990–1991 Iraqi forces invade Kuwait, leading to the Gulf War. While Iraqi forces are fighting the U.S.-led coalition, Kurds in northern Iraq revolt. Iraqi troops crush the revolt, and thousands of Kurds flee to Iran and Turkey. Operation Provide Comfort is established. Military operations against the PKK continue, with Turkish soldiers attacking PKK bases in Iraq.

1992 The Kurdistan Front establishes a government in northern Iraq and holds elections. The KDP and the PUK agree to govern the region together.

1993–1994 The PKK declares a unilateral cease-fire and drops demands for Kurdish independence. After President Ozal dies, the negotiations end and the conflict resumes.

1996 The KDP, with the help of Iraqi troops, defeats the PUK. The Kurdish safe haven collapses, and thousands of PUK fighters and Kurdish civilians flee to the Iranian border.

1998–1999 Kurdish security forces arrest Abdullah Ocalan in Kenya. The Turkish court sentences Ocalan to death.

SELECTED BIBLIOGRAPHY

Bulloch, John, and Harvey Morris. *No Friends but the Mountains: The Tragic History of the Kurds.* London: Viking, 1991.

Chaliand, Gerard, ed. *A People without a Country: The Kurds and Kurdistan.* New York: Olive Branch Press, 1993.

Kashi, Ed. *When the Borders Bleed: The Struggle of the Kurds.* New York: Pantheon Books, 1994.

Laizer, Sheri. *Into Kurdistan: Frontiers under Fire.* London: Zed Books Ltd., 1991.

McDowall, David. *A Modern History of the Kurds.* London: I.B. Taurus, 1996.

O'Ballance, Edgar. *The Kurdish Struggle, 1920–1994.* New York: St. Martins Press, 1996.

O'Connor, Karen. *A Kurdish Family.* Minneapolis: Lerner Publications Company, 1996.

INDEX

ABOUT THE AUTHOR

Kari J. Bodnarchuk is a journalist, editor, and adventurer who has traveled to 30 countries in Africa, Asia, Europe, North America, and the South Pacific. While working as an editor and reporter for a Massachusetts newspaper group, Kari developed and ran a Rwanda relief effort to collect clothing and money for medicines. She traveled to Rwanda in 1994 to report on the distribution of these supplies in refugee camps and hospitals around Rwanda and eastern Zaire. Kari now writes for newspapers and magazines and runs classes on adventure travel. She is also the author of Lerner Publications' *Rwanda: Country Torn Apart*.

ABOUT THE CONSULTANTS

Andrew Bell-Fialkoff, *World in Conflict* series consultant, is a specialist on nationalism, ethnicity, and ethnic conflict. He is the author of *Ethnic Cleansing*, published by St. Martin's Press in 1996, and has written numerous articles for foreign affairs and other journals. He is writing a book on the role of migration in the history of the Eurasian Steppe. Mr. Bell-Fialkoff lives in Bradford, Massachusetts.

Dr. Vera Saeedpour is the founder and director of the Kurdish Library and Museum in Brooklyn, New York.

SOURCES OF QUOTED MATERIAL

p. 14 Vera Saeedpour, founder and director of the Kurdish Library and Museum, Brooklyn, NY, and collected from *Kurdish Studies, An International Journal*, The Kurdish Library, Vol. 8, Numbers 1 and 2, 1995, http://burn.ecsd.edu/%7Earchive/kurd-l/1995/0031.html; p. 27 U.S. State Department Country Report on Turkey, http://www.hri.org/docs/USSD-Rights/94/Turkey94.html; p. 30 1995 Food and Agriculture Organization (FAO) and World Food Program (WFP) report; p.30 United Nations Department of Humanitarian Affairs; p. 45 John Bulloch and Harvey Morris, *No Friends But the Mountains: The Tragic History of the Kurds* (New York: Oxford University Press, 1992), p. 88; p. 63 Declaration of June 29, John Bulloch and Harvey Morris, *No Friends But the Mountains: The Tragic History of the Kurds* (New York: Oxford University Press, 1992), p. 128; pp. 63–64 Gerard Chaliand, ed., *A People Without A Country: The Kurds and Kurdistan* (New York: Olive Branch Press, 1933), p. 152, p. 152; p. 67 Gerard Chaliand, ed., *A People Without A Country: The Kurds and Kurdistan* (New York: Olive Branch Press, 1933), p. 168; p. 82 Aliza Marcus' from "Turkish Writer Goes on Trial," in Kurdish News, #17 – June 1995, printed by the Kurdistan Committee of Canada, http://burn.ucsd.edu/~.../kurd-1/1995/0151.html, and Eric Avebury, Parliamentary Human Rights Group Chairman, "Turkey's Kurdish Policy in the Nineties," a paper presented at the Middle East Studies Association, Washington D.C., December 1995, http://www.kurdistan.org/Articles/d1.html; p. 85 Speech to the Turkish Grand National Assembly, June 30, 1995, Basbakanlik Basimevi, Ankara. (Reproduced, in part, by Eric Avebury, Parliamentary Human Rights Group Chairman, "Turkey's Kurdish Policy in the Nineties," a paper presented at the Middle East Studies Association, Washington D.C., December 1995, http://www.kurdistan.org/Articles/d1.html; p. 86 "Kurdistan? Which one do you mean?", *The Economist*, August 10, 1996, p. 29; p. 88 Suleyman Demirel, Reuters, Oct. 7, 1997 and Associated Press, Dec. 27, 1997; p. 89 http://dailynews.yahoo.com/headlines/ts/story.html?s=v/nm/19990629/ts/turkey_ocalan_5.html; p. 94 "American Hammers, Kurdish Nails," by Jon Stewart, in the San Francisco Chronicle, Feb. 11, 1996, see http://burn.ucsd.edu/%Eakin/hammers.html; p. 94: :60 Minutes: 'An American Dilemma,'" Vol. XXVIII, No. 16, January 14, 1996, http://burn.ucsd.edu%Eakin/dilemma.html; p. 96: Mehdi Zana, Washington Kurdish Institute Kurdish Conflict Resolution Forum, Summary and Recommendations, see http://www.clark.net/kurd/ReportKCRF.html.